JANE'S 1982-83
MILITARY REVIEW

JANE'S 1982-83 MILITARY REVIEW

edited by Ian V. Hogg

Second year of issue

JANE'S

First published in 1982 by
Jane's Publishing Company Limited
238 City Road, London EC1V 2PU

ISBN 0 7106 0218 9

Computer Typesetting by Method Ltd
Woodford Green, Essex

Printed in Great Britain by
Mackays of Chatham

Publisher's note
The first compilation in this series, published in October 1981, was issued under the title *Jane's Military Annual 1981-82.*

Photograph credits

Page 10: Aérospatiale; pages 12–18 inclusive: Press Association; pages 24–25: Ian V. Hogg; page 26: Fabrique Nationale Herstal Photographie; pages 26–27: General Dynamics; page 40: US Department of State; page 45: Austin J. Brown; pages 46–47: British Aerospace; pages 48–49 upper: Rockwell International; pages 48–49 lower: Aérospatiale; page 53 upper: MBB; page 54: US Army; pages 59–65: Anna Hogg; page 66: Ian V. Hogg; pages 67–69: Pilkington; page 70 upper: Benmuir Photographic Services Limited; pages 70–71 lower: Officine Galileo; page 71 upper: Euromissile; page 72: Euromissile; page 73 left: Texas Instruments Inc; page 73 middle right: Philips Usfa B.V.; page 73 bottom right: Philips Usfa B.V.; page 75 upper: HK; page 75 lower: Valmet Oy; page 76: Ian V. Hogg; page 79 upper: Ian V. Hogg; page 80 right: General Defence Corporation; pages 82–83: Crown Copyright; page 84: F. R. Logan; pages 85–87: via G. Tillotson; page 88 left: Rheinmetall GmbH; pages 88–89 upper: Rheinmetall GmbH; pages 88–89 lower: via G. Tillotson; page 90 upper: GIAT; page 90 right: via G. Tillotson; page 91 left: Hayman Studio of Commercial Photography; page 91 upper right: via Christopher Foss; page 91 lower right: via Christopher Foss; pages 92–93: via G. Tillotson; pages 94–95: via Tillotson/Foss; pages 97–101: West German MoD; pages 102–103: London News Service; pages 104–105: West German MoD; pages 107–123: NATO CENTAG; page 124: US Army; page 125 upper: Teledyne; page 125 lower: Krauss-Maffei; page 126: US Army; page 127 upper: Panhard; page 127 lower: Hagglund and Soner; page 128 top: MoD; page 128 middle & lower: Bofors; page 129: GIAT; page 130: MATRA; page 131 top: FVV Ordnance Division; page 131 middle: HK; page 131 bottom: General Dynamics; page 134: Rheinstahl Henschel AG; page 135: Ian V. Hogg; page 139 top: US Army; page 139 lower: GKN-Sankey; page 141 lower: US Army; pages 142–143: Ian V. Hogg; page 144: Anna Hogg; page 146: US Army; page 149: via Ian V. Hogg; page 150: Ian V. Hogg; page 151: via Ian V. Hogg; page 152: Ian V. Hogg; pages 153–160: Canadian MoD.

Cover: First shown at the 1982 British Army Equipment Exhibition was the Universal turret version of the Vickers Valiant MBT, equipped in this instance with the L11 series 120 mm rifled gun developed by the Royal Ordnance Factory, Nottingham. (Photo: *Brian Cooke/Szwed Doman Associates for Vickers Defence Systems*)

Contents

The Military Year
Ian V. Hogg 7

Afghanistan, the Unending Struggle
David C. Isby 28

Air Power, the Falklands and the Future
John W. R. Taylor 45

Pictures from the British Army Equipment Exhibition, 1982 58

Optronics
Charles Castle 66

Explosives and Ammunition, the State of the Art
Ian V. Hogg 74

Tank Guns for Future Main Battle Tanks
Geoffrey Tillotson 82

The German Territorial Army
J. A. English 96

Central Army Group, Pillar of NATO Defence
J. A. English 107

New Equipment 124

The Roles of Infantry in the Manoeuvre Battle
Richard Simpkin 132

One Hundred Years Ago
Ian V. Hogg 148

The Current State of the NATO Alliance
Nicholas Stethem 153

Foreword

The 1981–82 *Jane's Military Annual* broke new ground in providing a review of current military thought and opinion, and was well received by our public. For this 1982–83 edition we have made some changes. The title is now that of 'Review' rather than 'Annual', and we have omitted the year; these changes have been made in order to lessen the risk of confusion between this and other annual publications under the Jane's imprint. We have also made some small changes in layout in order to make the finished book more attractive. As before, we have cast a wide net to include articles on a variety of contemporary military subjects, pictures of new equipment, and records of military happenings during the past year. We have endeavoured to make the final mixture one of wide appeal, and we would solicit the comments of readers on the result.

I.V.H

The Contributors

Ian Hogg has spent the majority of his life as a soldier, seeing active service all over the world. He is technically trained and on retiring from the Artillery he has become a freelance writer and an authority on gunnery subjects. He has written more than 40 books and has lost count of the magazine articles which he has had published.

John English is a serving officer in the Canadian Ground Forces and an infantryman. He has written a scholarly book on the subject of infantry and is currently researching another. He is presently serving in the Canadian Ministry of Defence.

David Isby is a Washington-based legislative assistant specialising in defence affairs. He is the author of *Weapons and Tactics of the Soviet Army*.

A specialist during his service on armoured fighting vehicle policy, **Brigadier (Retired) R. E. Simpkin** OBE MC FBIM MIL MTG retired early to build a second career on authorship, translation and language-related consultancy. His publications on mechanised warfare include *Tank Warfare* (1979), *Mechanised Infantry* (1980) and *Antitank 90* (1981) as well as numerous articles.

Nicholas Stethem is an ex-infantry officer of the Canadian Army. He is now the Director of the Strategic Analysis Group in Toronto and is an adviser to the Canadian Government and CBS on defence-related matters.

John W. R. Taylor FRAeS, FRHIstS, FSLAET, began his aviation career in 1941 as a member of Sir Sydney Camm's wartime fighter design team at Hawker Aircraft Ltd. He has led for 21 years the team responsible for *Jane's All the World's Aircraft*, the bible of the aerospace industry, and delights in the fact that this has brought him good friends and colleagues in every aircraft-manufacturing country on Earth. The 214 books bearing his name, published in more than twelve languages, include everything from spotters' handbooks to an award-winning history of the RAF Central Flying School and a history of aviation of which more than 280,000 copies have been sold worldwide.

Geoffrey Tillotson is a British Army officer who specialised during his service in vehicle design and the problems associated with AFVs. He is currently involved in a post relating to the safety of fuels and explosives and his spart-time activity is as a military writer. He is a contributor to *Jane's Armour and Artillery*, and has written several magazine articles on this subject.

The Military Year

Ian V. Hogg

Writing as we are in June 1982, the military thought uppermost in everyone's mind must be the campaign recently and successfully concluded by British forces in the Falkland Islands. A real analysis of the campaign cannot be done until full reports are in and made public, and a running analysis has been made difficult by the paucity of hard information. The daily press, in the lack of anything better, filled pages with speculation, but from our viewpoint we would be better occupied in reviewing the performance so far revealed, both the performance of the weapons and the performance of the troops.

So far as the latter goes the activities of Royal Marine Commandos, Paratroops and Infantry of the Line, Artillery, Cavalry and service troops has been exemplary. The whole campaign has proved that regular soldiers properly trained can operate in any conditions and produce satisfactory results. Any doubt of the efficiency of the contemporary British Soldier was dispelled in one example by the performance of the 2nd Battalion, The Parachute Regiment, at Goose Green when 600 men sustained 17 casualties in killing 250 and capturing 1400 Argentines. The figures alone will go down in history as one of the most astonishing feats of arms ever recorded, and when account is taken of the climatic conditions under which these men fought, even

The 84 mm Carl Gustaf anti-tank recoilless gun in action

more credit will accrue to them.

Similarly, the amazing cross-country ability of the Royal Marine Commandos in their advance on Port Stanley was an eye-opener to those who had claimed that the advance would be slow because there was only one road and because the ground was too soft to sustain wheeled vehicles. There were also dismal forecasts after the cargo ship *Atlantic Conveyor* was sunk along with numbers of Chinook helicopters with which the land forces were to be lifted. None of this dismayed the Commandos, who shouldered their enormous packs and set off on foot at a pace which would kill lesser men,

The Short 'Blowpipe' man-portable supersonic anti-aircraft missile which gave a good account of itself in the Falklands campaign

British troops and their Volvo over-snow vehicles disembarking from a landing craft during an exercise in Norway. It was this training which gave the British troops an enormous advantage over their opponents in the Falklands

to arrive on the heights overlooking Port Stanley in a time which completely threw the opposition. They were ably supported in their advanced position by 105 mm light guns of the 29 (Cdo) Field Regiment RA which had been helicopter-lifted through appalling weather conditions into positions from which they could give fire support and completely dominate the Argentine positions.

At the time of writing few names of individuals have become available, and it would be invidious to single out any particular person for praise until the whole story is known. Nevertheless, we feel it only fair to commend the action of the unknown Royal Marine who, during the initial invasion by the Argentine forces, turned his Carl Gustaf anti-tank gun on to first a helicopter and then an Argentinian naval frigate, both with some measure of success. We doubt if either role had ever crossed the weapon designer's mind, but Marines were never people to be constrained by solely theoretical considerations, and the versatility of both the man and his weapon were in the highest traditions of the Corps.

An interesting feature of the campaign, but one which will probably never be fully revealed, has been the involvement of the Special Air Service and the Special Boat Service. The SAS has largely, in the public's eye, been seen as a counter-terrorist force, and it is gratifying that they should have been shown in their 'proper' role as an adjunct to the field forces. Though few details are available it is known that units were put ashore on the islands some time before the arrival of the main British invading force and acted in a reconnaissance role, determining the Argentine Order of Battle; they then acted as guides when the main force landed. There have also been rumours of a small party landed in mainland Argentine to sabotage in particular AM 39 Exocet carrying Super Etendard naval strike aircraft.

The existence of the Special Boat Service appeared as a surprise to many of the general public, who had little idea that such a force existed. As with the SAS their activities appear to have been in reconnaissance and guiding roles, though there is a persistent rumour that one reason for the non-appearance of the Argentine Navy was that several of their vessels had been attacked with limpet mines in their anchorages and were unfit to put to sea as a result. This is another nebulous area which will probably never be resolved.

The performance of equipment is the subject which has attracted the attention of most professional army-watchers. Much of the weaponry used in the Falklands had never been put to the test of war, having been adopted into service solely on the results of trials against artificial targets. That so much of the equipment has come through without complaint is a matter for congratulation for those responsible for its design, development and procurement. All too often the speed of adoption of weapons appears to be so slow as to be incomprehensible, as authority vies with authority in demanding more tests, a re-design here, a change there, yet more tests, and so on until the eventual adoption is practically an anti-climax. Yet as the campaign has shown, it is such painstaking perfectionism which ensures that the weapon really does what it claims, does it all day, and does it in the vilest possible conditions. The performance of Rapier has justified everyone's faith in it, and it was noticeable that the results got better as they went along; no wonder, since we are sure that the operators fired more missiles in their first twenty-four hours ashore than they had in all their previous service. This has always been a disputed point in the question of training, that operators simply never had sufficient experience with the live missile, due to cost, and therefore had to make do with simulators for most of their time. That simulators pay off is now clear, and it has been reinforced by the results achieved with the Blowpipe anti-aircraft missile since this, in our

The Milan anti-tank missile fitted with the 'Mira' infra-red night sight unit

view, demands a higher level of skill than does the Rapier and, again, this skill is largely imparted by simulator training. Nevertheless, indications are that the operators of both types of weapon needed some time to 'get their eye in' before they began to achieve a good rate of results; good as simulators are they can never entirely substitute for the real thing, and the performance in a somnolent classroom trainer is not quite the same as trying to operate the same controls with aircraft screaming overhead, bombs and bullets flying and the adrenalin squirting out of your ears.

In the matter of basic infantry weapons both sides were evenly matched, armed with the FN FAL rifle and the FN MAG machine gun in 7.62 mm NATO calibre. The British artillery was somewhat at a disadvantage to the Argentine since it had only the 105 mm Light Gun whilst the Argentines used French 155 mm howitzers and the elderly American 105 mm M1 howitzer. The light gun fires a modern high-efficiency shell to 17,000 metres, while the M1 fires an old pattern of shell to 10,800 metres; the field guns were thus an uneven match, but this was counter-balanced by the longer reach and heavier shell of the Argentine 155 mm weapons. Their counter-battery capability would have been ample reason to deploy the British guns as far back as possible, but we gather that in fact, the gunners have been close up behind our own infantry, since the presence of the guns is more reassuring than the mere noise of them some distance to the rear. Support must not only be given it must be seen to be given, and the spirit of Le Cateau will be a long time dying.

The Blues & Royals acted as the armoured reconnaissance force with their Scorpion and Scimitar light tanks. These vehicles are particularly well-suited to this type of terrain, since their ground pressure is some 0.39 kg/sq cm, less than that of a well-laden foot soldier, and they can skate over soft ground with an alacrity which no other tracked vehicle can approach – even the Volvo Bv202 articulated over-snow carriers have a heavier ground pressure. The Argentine armour on the island appears to have been little more than a handful of Panhard armoured cars, some APCs and a number of LVTP-7 amphibians which were used in the initial landings. These scarcely constituted a viable mobile armoured force in the face of Scorpions armed with 76 mm guns, and it is not surprising that there was no attempt to use them in any combat role.

The one thing which might have caused the Blues & Royals some trouble was the possible employment of anti-tank missiles against them. The Argentines were said to have numbers of Cobra, Bantam and SS12 missiles at their disposal. These are all 'first-generation'

The Falklands Campaign

The campaign in the Falkland Islands was brought to a successful conclusion just as these pages were being prepared for the printer, and therefore we have been unable to prepare a carefully-reasoned analysis of the affair. In default, therefore, we present a selection of photographs from official sources, together with a map outlining the main course of the action. We hope to be able to publish a full account in our next year's edition.

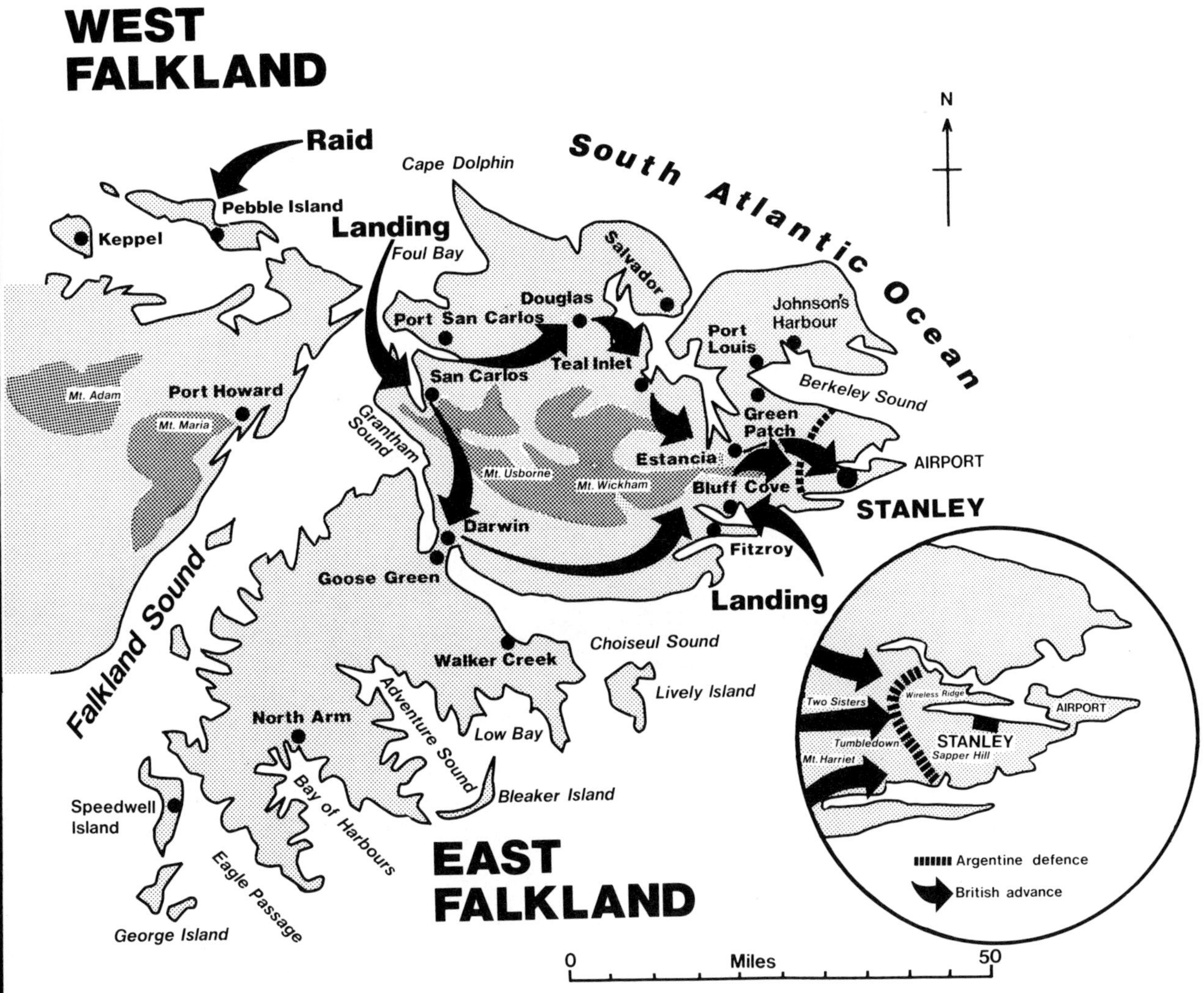

The Falklands

(Below) Ascension Island acted as the forming-up area and allowed troops to obtain some firing practice before going on to the Falklands

(Bottom) Soldiers of the 3rd Bn The Parachute Regiment, ashore from *Canberra*, carrying out live firing on Ascension Island during their stop en route to the Falklands

A practice run for a Royal Marine commando raiding party

The Falklands

(Right) Troops of the 5th Infantry Brigade boarding a Royal Marine landing craft for the final leg of their 8000 mile voyage to the Falkland Islands

(Below) Argentine troops who died in the battle for Goose Green awaiting burial

HMS *Sir Galahad* ablaze after an Argentine air raid at Bluff Cove

The Falklands

(Right) Survivors come ashore

(Below) Wounded from the *Sir Galahad* are brought ashore by helicopter

The Falklands

(Right) The Instrument of Surrender

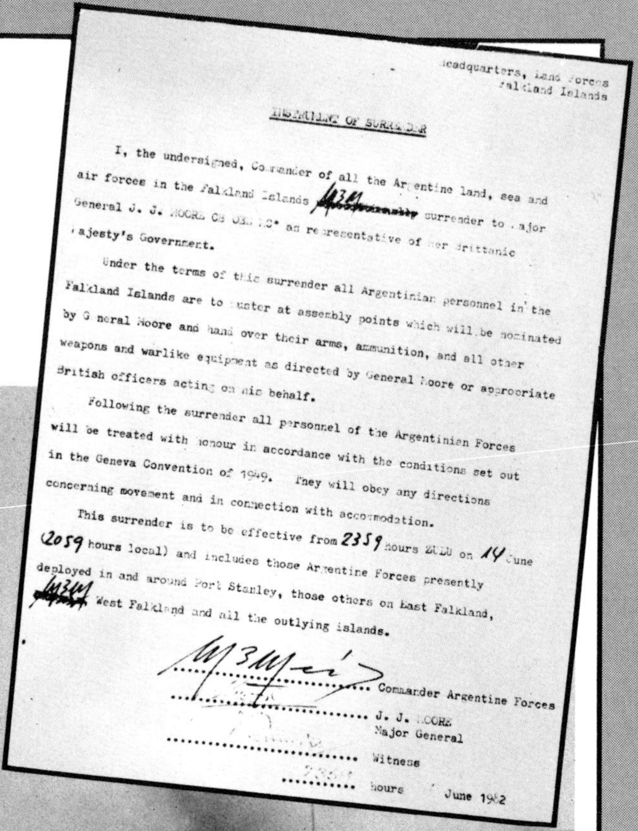

Headquarters, Land Forces
Falkland Islands

INSTRUMENT OF SURRENDER

I, the undersigned, Commander of all the Argentine land, sea and air forces in the Falkland Islands surrender to Major General J. J. MOORE CB OBE MC* as representative of Her Brittanic Majesty's Government.

Under the terms of this surrender all Argentinian personnel in the Falkland Islands are to muster at assembly points which will be nominated by General Moore and hand over their arms, ammunition, and all other weapons and warlike equipment as directed by General Moore or appropriate British officers acting on his behalf.

Following the surrender all personnel of the Argentinian Forces will be treated with honour in accordance with the conditions set out in the Geneva Convention of 1949. They will obey any directions concerning movement and in connection with accommodation.

This surrender is to be effective from 2359 hours ZULU on 14 June (2059 hours local) and includes those Argentine Forces presently deployed in and around Port Stanley, those others on East Falkland, West Falkland and all the outlying islands.

.... Commander Argentine Forces

.... J. J. MOORE
Major General

.... Witness

.... hours June 1982

(Below) The after section of *Sir Galahad* ablaze. The Brigade of Guards, who were about to disembark, suffered heavily in this attack

designs which have to be manually steered to their destination, a feat which demands considerable skill and dedication – requisites which might not have been forthcoming. The majority of the Argentinian force defending Port Stanley were short-service conscripts, in which case few of them were likely to have had anything like the amount of training needed to make a proficient operator. The 1973 'Yom Kippur' war proved that a burst of machine gun fire in the vicinity of the operator is usually enough to distract his attention sufficiently for him to lose control of the missile. However, the situation never arose, and the British armoured forces were (fortunately) denied the chance of seeing what these weapons could do.

British troops were provided with Milan missiles, 84 mm Carl Gustaf and 120 mm Wombat RCL guns and 66 mm LAW rockets as their anti-armour weapons, but none appear to have seen employment in their primary role. On the other hand there were several reports of the use of Milan, the 84 mm RCL and the 66 mm LAW as point target weapons to deal with machine gun posts and the like form of 'battlefield obstacle'. There has always been a minority demand for anti-personnel missiles for this type of weapon and we would think that this school of thought has been strengthened in their beliefs as a result of these actions. A Milan missile is, it may be thought, an expensive way of removing two men and a machine gun, but when one considers the potential for mischief that a well-emplaced machine gun has, particularly in such open country as obtained in the Falklands, then the exchange is obviously worth every penny.

All in all the Falklands campaign has underlined the virtues of good generalship, fit, well-trained and well-disciplined soldiers, good equipment and sound basic tactics and military sense. It has always been considered that to take a defended position required a superiority in the order of three to one in both men and equipment, and to complete such a campaign under the handicaps of a negative strength ratio, a hostile climate and a supply line some 8000 miles long says volumes for the quality of the attacking force. Without wishing to sound harsh, we have to say that the Army appears to be the only service to come out of this campaign without a black mark of any sort against it.

The rest of the world has, of course, seen its share of wars during the past year, wars which have been infinitely more destructive than the affair in the South Atlantic. The most recent eruption has been the Israeli invasion of the Lebanon with the avowed intention of driving out the guerrillas of the Palestine Liberation Organisation which have been using that unhappy country as their base for several years. Had the Israeli forces stopped at their declared aim of clearing a 25-Mile 'sanitized zone' north of their border, so as to inhibit PLO parties using the area to emplace weapons, few would probably have argued with them, but in the true Wildean spirit of 'nothing succeeds like excess' they have gone further and intend, at the time of writing, to clear the entire Lebanon of PLO at, apparently, any cost. However many PLO may or may not have been killed so far, there is little doubt that tens of thousands of innocent Lebanese have been killed, wounded or rendered homeless and it seems probable that the final tally will be yet greater. Material damage has been immense, the city of Beirut being virtually laid waste and lesser towns such as Sidon and Tyre severely battered. Israel may gain militarily from this war, but we feel that it has lost a great deal of goodwill in many parts of the world.

A short distance away from this war, the conflict between Iran an Iraq has reached a surprising conclusion. A year ago most observers would not have given a great deal for Iran's chances; it was, they said, internally divided; the Shah's professional army had been shredded, most of its better officers purged, the equipment left to rust, regiments disbanded on grounds of suspect ideology and so forth. This sort of fragmented force would be no match for the Iraqis, a cohesive army with good motivation which would sweep through Iran, topple the Ayatollah's regime and restore some sort of normality. But somehow it didn't work out that way. As history has often told us, external threats do wonders in uniting a fragmented country and this is what has happened to Iran. After initial setbacks the army found its feet, new leadership appeared, and the Iraqis were pushed back across the ground they had gained, lost Khorramshahr, and were eventually ejected from Iran and thrust firmly beyond their own border. This, unfortunately, has led the Iranians to assume a degree of military expertise which they do not actually possess, and this has given rise to some political proclamations which may yet cause more unrest. The fact that they have defeated the Iraqi forces has led the Iranians to assume that they are now the chosen leaders of the Moslem world and they have lost little time in telling the rest of the Arab nations how they should conduct their affairs in future. We fear that we have not heard the last of Iran in their new role of military experts.

The Soviet campaign in Afghanistan appears to have settled down to a desultory guerrilla war. The occupying force has held its control of Kabul and the surrounding area and has maintained communications routes to other towns and back into Soviet territory, but it appears not to have made any effort to try and occupy the entire country or to bring it all under control, remaining content to secure the strategically vital areas and letting the guerrillas roam as they will outside those areas. In short, it has come up against the same intractable problem which confronted the British and Indian Armies in those parts fifty and more years ago and has settled for more or less the same solution. The way of the empire-builder has never been an easy one.

What is more alarming are the frequent reports of chemical warfare which have come out of Afghanistan and also out of Laos and Cambodia. The reports are sometimes vague, sometimes detailed, but they do appear to have several points of similarity, most speaking of 'yellow rain' which is dispersed from aerial bombs and then apparently activated by firing a rocket into the cloud. The physiological effects run the gamut of internal bleeding, apparent nervous damage, hallucinations, coma and death. Because of the transient nature of chemical attacks and the isolation of the areas, it has never been possible to get a reliable and trained observer to the spot in order to carry out scientific tests – the 'smoking gun' concept as the Americans call it. Nevertheless, there seems to be sufficient correlation between the various reports to suggest that some form of mycotoxin is being used and that Soviet technology is behind it. The Soviets have long been assumed to have a highly developed CBW capability, in spite of sundry treaties and agreements to the contrary, and their level of troop protection and preparedness is testimony to the seriousness with which they view CBW as a threat.

The reports in past years have puzzled scientists, since they appeared to combine the effects of several known chemical agents into one, but in 1981 some plant specimens were obtained from the Thailand/Cambodia border, where Vietnamese aircraft had delivered a chemical attack, and these were followed up by water and soil samples all of which indicated that they had been sprayed with 'T2 Toxin' or tricothecene. Much of the published research work on this substance has been performed in the USSR, since it can occur naturally on diseased grain and in the 1930s had killed numbers of Russian people. But the levels of toxin found in Cambodia were some 20 times the natural level, suggesting that its presence was no accident. Moreover the physiological effects of T2 and the 'yellow rain' are similar. The evidence so far is scarcely enough to warrant the American assertion that they had actually found the 'smoking gun' at the scene of the crime, and, not unexpectedly, it was roundly denounced by the Soviets as a capitalist lie. Equally predictably a United Nations Commission were denied facilities to visit the affected countries and make an investigation, so the

whole affair remains in the realms of speculation. But without doubt something is killing Afghans, Laotians and Cambodians in a particularly unpleasant way and it is to be hoped that Western agencies concerned with CBW are taking due notice.

The Reagan administration in the USA has taken steps to reactivate a chemical warfare plant and prepare production of 'binary' CW agents for use in artillery shells and aerial bombs. More outcry has been raised however by the decision to go ahead with the preparation of enhanced radiation weapons – the so-called 'neutron bomb' – for use in rocket and missile warheads and in artillery projectiles. More nonsense has been talked about this weapon than about any other which has appeared in the last thirty years, and much of the opposition has been a godsend to Soviet propaganda. Some of the argument has been so loose as to be ludicrous, as, for example the submission that neutrons are a form of gas and therefore forbidden under chemical warfare treaties. Much has also been made of the weapon's property of killing without excessive blast and destruction of material, suggesting that it is a capitalist weapon to preserve property at the expense of life. Another attacking point has been the emotive use of the word 'bomb', suggesting that it is a weapon to be used against the civilian population so as to exterminate them without damaging their cities which, presumably, will then be available for looting.

All these arguments conveniently fudge the issue, which is simply that the enhanced radiation weapon is a tactical device, for short range use, and specifically intended as a counter to massive armoured attacks in

The Vickers GBT 155 self-propelled gun turret, seen on display at the British Army Equipment Exhibition, 1982, at Aldershot

Central Europe. In view of the much-quoted Soviet superiority in tank strength, the enhanced radiation weapon offers the NATO forces their only hope of stopping a major Soviet armoured thrust before it over-runs them. It has no validity as an attacking weapon, nor as a strategic weapon, and the objections to it are raised purely on the grounds that if NATO possesses it, then NATO can defend itself successfully against massed armour. This, in the Soviet view, constitutes an unfair advantage, and therefore the propaganda stops have been pulled out to their fullest extent in order to keep NATO weak.

Moving now to consider more conventional types of weapon, 1981/2 has seen the unveiling of a few interesting projects. Most of them are 'private ventures' by the major companies in the defence industry and it will be interesting to see how they fare in the open market at which most of them are aimed.

For some years the 'private venture' manufacture of artillery has been dormant; this has been due to a variety of causes, among them the role of state arsenals in producing artillery, the quantity of redundant artillery which has been released by the major nations, the quantity of artillery which has been made available under military aid programmes, and, of course, the enormous expense of research and development in this area. But although most of the smaller countries have been happy to accept aid weapons or to adopt older designs discarded by the major armies, there comes a time when nothing but the best will do, and there also comes a time when the artillerymen of the smaller countries master their craft sufficiently to realise that there are gaps in their armoury which are unlikely to be filled by benevolent friends. We now seem to be reaching this point, and thus the private gunmakers are beginning to stir once more, seeing various holes in the market which they might profitably fill.

One of the bigger gaps is in the provision of medium-calibre self-propelled artillery – particularly the ubiquitous 155 mm howitzer. There are, it is true, several designs available and one or two more under development. There is the American M109, found all over the world, and the forthcoming SP70 tri-national development. But the M109 is now rather old and cannot easily adapt to more modern types of projectile, while the SP70, when it comes, is undoubtedly going to be fearsomely expensive, complicated, and difficult to maintain.

Reasoning from this, OTO-Melara of Italy have produced an economical 155 mm self-propelled howitzer using the chassis and hull of their OT-40 medium tank (another private venture design) allied to a turret carrying a 41-calibre howitzer based on a design developed several years ago as a possible replacement barrel for M109s in Italian service. It has a muzzle brake and fume extractor and used a screw breech mechanism. Traverse and elevation are hydraulically controlled, with manual option, and there is also the option of hand or automatic loading. The Italian Simmel company has developed a range of ammunition specially for this howitzer, which includes conventional high explosive, illuminating and base ejection smoke shells, plus base-bleed and rocket-assisted long range projectiles. The conventional shell has a maximum range of 24 km; the base-bleed shell will reach to 27.5 km and the rocket-assisted shell is said to reach 30 km. 200 of these howitzers have been ordered by a Middle Eastern country and further orders are expected.

More recently the Vickers Shipbuilding and Engineering Company have announced their 'GBT-155 Fighting System', which is a turret and 40-calibre 155 mm howitzer produced as a unit which can be fitted into the hull of any suitable medium or heavy tank, replacing the original turret. In this way redundant or

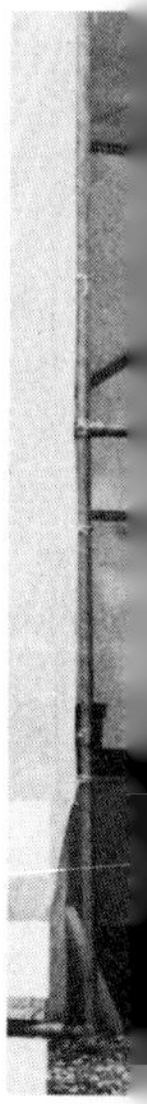

obsolescent tanks can be turned into efficient self-propelled howitzers at minimum cost. In addition, of course, the unit could be incorporated into a suitable hull and built as an SP gun, and Vickers have recently shown such a design using the hull of the Vickers Mark III medium tank as the basis.

Private venture has also been responsible for a number of light armoured vehicles which have appeared within the last year, mostly aimed at the APC/MICV area, (armoured personnel carrier/mechanized infantry combat vehicle). The British company GKN-Sankey have publicly shown their MCV-80, developed for the British Army and it is

(Left) The GKN-Sankey 'Simba' wheeled AFV mounting a 90 mm Cockerill gun

(Below) MCV-80, the GKN-Sankey armoured combat vehicle under development for the British Army

scheduled to enter service within the next three years or so. This vehicle weighs in at about 24 tonnes, carries ten men plus the driver and vehicle commander, and has a turret mounting a 30mm Rarden cannon and a 7.62 mm Hughes Chain Gun machine gun. There are also designs for a number of variant models, such as command, recovery, combat repair and mortar vehicles, all based on the same basic chassis and hull. This is an Army-sponsored development, but the company have also, on their own account, developed a four-wheeled armoured vehicle, the 'Simba', which appears to have enormous potential. In its simplest form this can be a wheeled APC, again carrying ten men plus the two-man crew; but it can also support such armament as an anti-aircraft cannon, a 20 mm ground cannon, anti-tank guided missile launchers, or even a low-pressure 90 mm gun, all within a weight of about 10 tonnes. And, also as a private move, GKN-Sankey have investigated the possibility of using the MCV-80 hull as the basis for a gun-carrying fighting vehicle; both 90 mm and 105 mm guns have been suggested, and when one considers that the German Krauss-Maffei company developed the Argentine TAM tank by putting a 105 mm gun turret on to the body of the German 'Marder' APC, which is of similar size and weight to MCV-80, then these suggestions make a good deal of sense.

One of the most important military vehicle programmes in view at the moment is the search by the US Marine Corps for a 'Light Armored Vehicle', a search which is producing some surprising answers. This search has arisen because the Rapid Deployment Force lacks lightweight, high-mobility armour and there is a need for between 300 and 800 assault vehicles and APCs for the 1st Marine Brigade. Several vehicles were put forward as possible solutions, among them the Mowag 'Piranha', Cadillac-Gage 'Commando V-150', Arrowpointe 'Dragoon', Panhard ERC-90 'Sagaie', Bell 'Hydracobra' (actually the Brazilian 'Urutu' to be built under licence), Vought 'Wolverine' (actually the French AMX-10RC mounting a Rheinmetall 105 mm gun and turret), and the AM-General 'Gator' (actually the Renault-Saviem VAB). The one thing all these vehicles have in common is that they are wheeled, which seems to have come about because the specification laid down an upper weight limit of 15 tonnes, and there appeared to be no tracked fighting vehicle capable

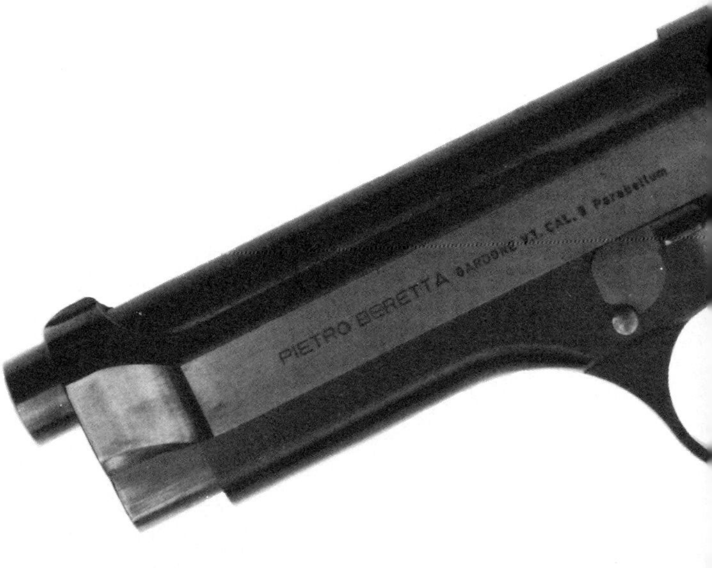

(Top) The Alvis 'Scorpion 90', currently under assessment for possible adoption by the US Marine Corps

(Above) The Beretta 92S automatic pistol, one of the better-fancied contenders for the American 9 mm pistol contest. Like all the other entries, it was rejected

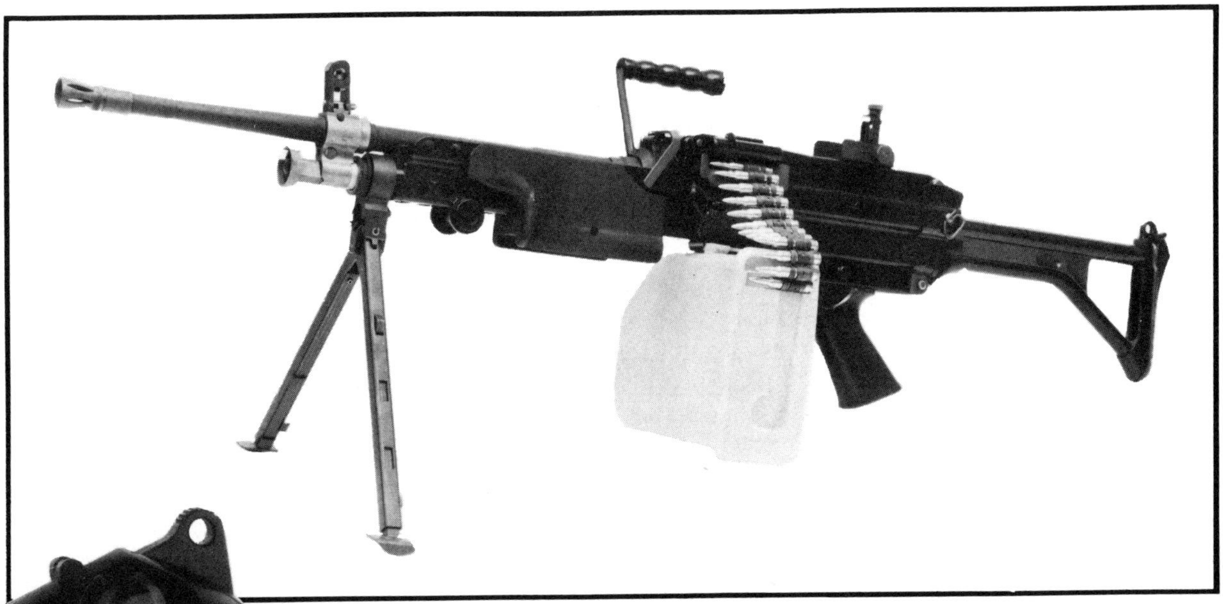

The 5.56 mm 'Minimi' machine gun, made by Fabrique Nationale of Belgium, has been formally adopted as a squad automatic weapon by the US Army

of making an impression inside that weight. Into this arena stepped Alvis of Coventry with their well-known Scorpion light tank, modified to carry a 90 mm gun and using a Perkins turb-charged diesel engine. This vehicle falls well within the weight limit, has a formidable performance which will see off virtually any wheeled vehicle in rough country and, unlike most of the others, can point (in its basic form) to a successful record in service with 14 armies and in combat with some. Since then Alvis have introduced their 'Stormer' APC, a lengthened and improved form of their earlier 'Spartan' and also fitted with the new Perkins diesel power unit, and this has been put forward to the US Marines as being a potential APC which would have the advantage of commonality of parts with the fighting vehicle if Scorpion 90 were to be selected. To give it the necessary fighting power, Stormer has been fitted with a turret by Arrowpointe (an American firm) which mounts the Hughes 25 mm Chain Gun cannon. Both the Alvis vehicles, together with vehicles from Cadillac-Gage and GM-Canada (ie the V-150 Commando and the Piranha) were exhaustively tested at the Marine test station at 29 Palms, California, from November 1981 to June 1982, and a decision is now awaited.

Another American trial which has caused some fluttering in the dovecotes has been their search for a new sidearm. The US Air Force started the ball rolling by deciding to replace their existing .45 M1911A1 automatic pistols and their varied inventory of .38 revolvers with a new 9 mm automatic pistol. The specification appears to have been somewhat loosely drawn, but the Air Force wanted a modern double-action weapon with a good-sized magazine. Several manufacturers throughout the world were invited to contribute, on the understanding that the selected weapon would have to be produced in the USA, and Smith & Wesson 459, Beretta 92S, Colt SSP, FN DA, FN GP35, Star M28, and Heckler & Koch VP70, PSP and P9S pistols were submitted for test.

By this time, however, the US Army had decided to come into the project. What happened next is not entirely clear, but the Department of Defense announced that it had thrown out all the Air Force test data since their tests had not been sufficiently scientific, and the whole project would be run again, presumably with more stringent rules. A period of silence then descended while the competing pistols were put

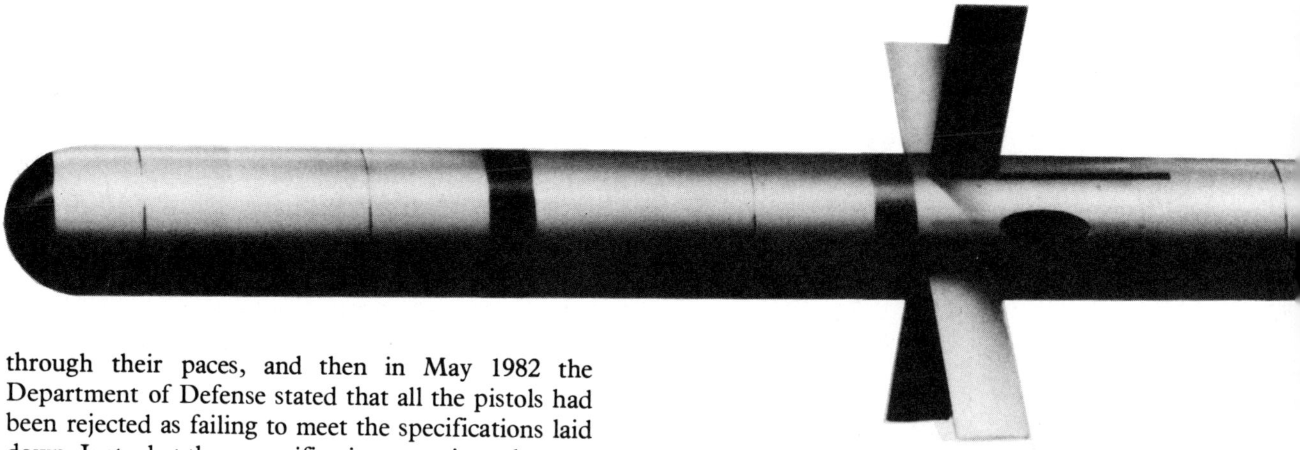

through their paces, and then in May 1982 the Department of Defense stated that all the pistols had been rejected as failing to meet the specifications laid down. Just what those specifications were is not known, but the DoD statement included the remark that 'all had failed to meet several of the 71 major design requirements' to which the obvious retort is that if there were so many major requirements, how many minor ones were there? How anyone can list 71 major requirements in such a relatively simple device as a pistol is a question in itself, and in view of the fact that several of the contestants are in military service throughout the world with success, it suggests that the specification tends towards the unrealistic. At present the whole project has been suspended. We cannot express much surprise over this; handguns are an emotive subject in the USA, and there appear to be numerous Congressmen and Senators taking a hand in the argument, largely in the interests of protecting the employment of their constituents. Anyone with the temerity to suggest that American soldiers should be armed with a foreign pistol was backing a loser before he started.

There is, however, some slight precedent; the US Army have adopted the FN MAG machine gun for use in tanks, and more recently they have approved the 5.56 mm FN 'Minimi' machine gun as a squad automatic weapon, though not without demanding so many modifications as to virtually make it a new model. This latter move is not before time, since the US Army has, over the years, been singularly unsuccessful in attempts to develop a native design of light machine gun. Why this should be, we cannot imagine; there has been no shortage of good designs in other countries, which suggests that there is nothing very difficult in producing an LMG, but in spite of that the GI has gone to war with the BAR, the .30 Browning air-cooled machine gun fitted with a butt and bipod, the Johnson and one or two other designs which have been more hindrance than help.

The eastern flow of the 'two-way street' continues unabated, among the most recent announcements being that the British Army may possibly become the first European user of the American 155 mm 'Copperhead' Cannon-Launched Guided Projectile. Trials of the projectile will take place at the Royal School of Artillery in September and October 1982; these will largely be concerned with evaluating the techniques of employment rather than passing technical judgement on the weapon. Provided it meets US Army reliability requirements and proves compatible with British communications and laser-guiding systems there is every chance that approval for its adoption will follow.

The Hughes 'Tank Breaker' missile, under development for the US Army, is among the first 'fire-and-forget' missiles, using an infra-red seeker to home on to its target

An artist's impression of the 'Terminally Guided Submissile' in action against tanks. The submissiles are ejected from artillery shells or rocket warheads and seek out individual targets, permitting armour concentrations to be attacked long before they reach the combat line

This will raise questions of partial manufacture in Britain, involving both private industry (for components) and the Royal Ordnance Factories organisation (for explosive filling and assembly of the complete weapon).

Copperhead illustrates the continuing interest in developing a wide variety of weapons – a golf bag full of different clubs as one authority put it – to counter armour, brought about by the continual presence of an estimated 10,000 MBTs in the Warsaw Pact forward elements. Whilst great reliance is placed on short-range weapons, more and more effort is going into developing munitions which can be launched by artillery or free-flight rocket so as to carry the fight to the tanks before they reach the forward edge of the battle area. This has led to several interesting designs of sub-munitions, dispensed from the major projectile, and intended to attack the relatively more vulnerable top surfaces of armoured vehicles. Hollow charge has been favoured in the past, but it is now being edged out by a related technique known as the 'self-forming fragment'. This is loosely based upon work done in the 1940s by Schardin in Germany and involves facing an explosive charge with a slightly concave plate of dense material. When the charge is detonated the plate is blown forward, being explosively-formed into a missile shape with sufficient penetrative power to go through top armour.

Having settled upon a method of attack, the problem then is to ensure that the weapon actually does attack a tank and various sensors, ranging from simple TV systems to infra-red and millimetric waves are being tried. In order to avoid the need for complex sub-munitions, laser guidance is relied upon to put the dispensing projectile above the target, relying upon the laws of chance to ensure that sufficient of the sub-munitions will actually strike. Another option is to fit the sub-munition with a parachute, rigged so as to cause it to spiral in such a manner that the sensor can scan a wide area during descent; should the sensor spot a target during this scan, electronic circuits can arrange for the charge to be detonated at the right portion of the next scan, so firing the forged fragment in the right direction.

It must be obvious by now that whatever the selected solution is going to be, one thing is certain; it will be expensive. Copperhead is said to cost $40,000 per copy, and this leads us to consider the rising prices of military equipment and wonder whether any army in the world is ever going to be able to afford what it needs. The bill for the Falklands campaign has been loosely calculated to be something in the order of £1800 million for a campaign of 74 days. This is roughly twice as much as the daily cost of World War Two for the British, and the forces involved were negligible in comparison to what was being fielded in 1944-45.

With main battle tanks costing in excess of £1 million, anti-aircraft tanks and self-propelled guns almost twice that price and the simplest missiles several tens of thousands of pounds, the prospect of putting together a modern army and giving it all the high-technology weapons which the manufacturers are busy developing is becoming a frightening proposition. During a recent meeting of the Royal Artillery Historical Society an officer related how, as a young subaltern, he had been in an observation post in Hong Kong directing the fire of coast artillery guns against the Japanese advancing through the New Territories in 1941. During the battle he was rung by his Battery Commander who said in an aggrieved tone, 'Look here, do you realise this ammunition costs £3 a shot? Just be careful . . .' Ah, for the days of innocence.

Afghanistan

The Unending Struggle

David C. Isby

All photographs by courtesy of Committee for a Free Afghanistan, Washington, D.C.

An Afghan combat group – armed with Lee-Enfields – returns home for re-supply

In the pre-dawn darkness of December 27, 1979, a column of BMD airborne infantry combat vehicles of the Soviet Army, manned by heavily armed paratroopers, moved out from their positions around Kabul airport. They may not have expected opposition at their objective – the Darulaman Palace outside Kabul, home of Afghanistan's Communist President, Hafizullah Amin – but Amin's guard resisted the start of their country's 'liberation'. A bitter firefight ensued until all eight of the Afghan's T-54 tanks were destroyed and President Amin put to death, the Soviets installing Barbak Karmal in his place.

As a result of this day's business, the Soviets found themselves, for the first time since 1945, involved in a war; not an insurgency, not a simple restoration of the Brezhnev Doctrine, but a fully-fledged and particularly brutal war. It is a war that is still going on today, and will probably be fought for some time to come yet. The war has not moderated in intensity since December 1979, when the Soviets decided to transform their presence from that of advisors and props to a Communist regime into that of invaders. Only those with access to highly classified intelligence know, in the West, the full course of the war, for the Soviets have revealed little in their open sources – until recently the involvement of Soviet troops was simply not mentioned.

The view from the Afghan side is also incomplete, being limited to glimpses where Western journalists have ventured or Afghans returned with information. Thus, while the Battle of Paghman in July 1981 and the Panjshir Valley offensive of August-September, 1981 are well known, other battles are not. The defeat of a large mechanized combined-arms force of Kabul regime troops in the Jedra district during a series of battles in June 1979 may have been the decisive event in forcing the Soviet invasion – at least many Afghans believe this to be so. Other battles, especially in the interior and the western regions of Afghanistan, have gone unreported. Little is known of the fighting near Herat, for example, except that it has been heavy and prolonged. Thus a thorough operational account of the war in Afghanistan is not possible. However, from what has emerged from the fighting, it is possible to draw a picture of the strategy, tactics, organization and weaponry of the Soviet war against Afghanistan.

The view from Kabul and Moscow, 1982

Afghanistan has known no peace since the 1978 coup brought in its wake a steadily escalating Soviet involvement. Today the Soviets are in position to wage a basically unending war if necessary. The Soviet war in Afghanistan is being run on the cheap. Testimony by the US Defense Intelligence Agency before Congress in September 1981 estimated that the Soviets spend only one to two per cent of their total defence expenditures on the war. They redeem some of the cost by billing the Kabul regime for their 'fraternal assistance', which is partially paid for in natural resources shipped to the Soviet Union.

The cost in Soviet lives has not been quite so cheap, but not prohibitive either. US State Department figures estimate 10-15 000 Soviet casualties by early 1982, about 5000 of which were killed. Other Western intelligence sources are not far from these figures. The Soviets suffered a number of defeats in 1980, with units as large as reinforced motorized rifle battalions being massacred by the Afghans. Though they no longer suffer defeats of this size, losses continue to mount.

The Soviet forces now in Afghanistan appear to consist of basically the same units that were involved in the 1979 invasion. The paratroopers of the 105th Guards Airborne Division (possibly reinforced to four to six rifle regiments in strength) are a strategic reserve and hold the vital Kabul-Bagram area. The 54th Motorized Rifle Division has apparently carried out

Always a heavy decentralized country, local groups have now taken over most government functions in the absence of influence of the Kabul regime. Here, Afghans provide transportation with a GAZ-63A truck

much of the fighting near Herat; and the 66th Motorized Rifle Division supports it in the Shindand-Farah sector (headquarters at Shindand). The 201st Motorized Rifle Division has the unenviable task of covering the Khyber pass, with headquarters at Jalalabad. The 360th Motorized Rifle Division is the Kabul garrison and has also apparently seen action in Wardak province. The 346th Motorized Rifle Division is in the Kandahar sector, the scene of fierce fighting throughout 1981 and in the spring of 1982 as the city changed hands several times.

The 5th Motorized Rifle Division is now reportedly in the Khanabad-Fezyabad sector, having possibly moved there from Farah. This may be linked to unconfirmed information that a new division, 16th Motorized Rifle, entered Afghanistan in 1981 with its headquarters at Mazar-e-Sharif. While there is uncertainty as to designations and deployments, there remains a total of seven or eight Soviet divisions. In addition, there are reportedly no less than five air assault brigades of three battalions each, which use helicopters for mobility. Controlling these activities is the equivalent of an army-level headquarters at Kabul. In addition to these forces, the Soviets can doubtlessly count on *Raydoviki* and *Vysotniki* unconventional warfare forces in Afghanistan. Units of the KGB Border Troops and MVD Internal troops have also been deployed in Afghanistan. Soviet air strength is estimated at 150 fixed-wing and 500-650 helicopters, which requires a substantial Air Force commitment. In addition, the Soviets have used a large number (estimated at 6000) of civilians who are working on restructuring the Afghan government and economy on the Soviet model.

The Soviet commitment is thus a considerable one. The number of troops deployed apparently well exceeds the 90-120 000 figure usually cited. Simply adding 90 per cent war establishment figures of the major combat units (at the smallest reported force) yields a strength of 80 000. To this must be added the non-divisional combat units, the support units, and headquarters. While some units – such as air

Lee-Enfield armed tribesmen with a captured T-34 – a tank still used by the Kabul regime. The hull and co-axial machineguns have already been salvaged by the guerrillas. The tank shows no signs of external damage and may have been surrendered by its crew

defence and radio-electronic combat – usually associated with Soviet formations may have been withdrawn, the long supply line may increase the number of support troops required. A figure of 135 000 soldiers would seem a reasonable minimum figure, not counting 'advisors' to the Kabul regime (an estimated 2000), the MVD and KGB or the civilian presence. The Air Force would certainly add at least 10 000 additional men to overall Soviet strength.

While the Soviets may be strong, the forces of the Kabul regime are weak. Their army, 80 000 strong in 1978, has been reduced to 25 000 through losses and wholesale desertions, often by complete subunits, to the guerrillas. The Afghan Army apparently still operates a large number of battalion and brigade-size divisions throughout the country. Press reports have placed the 7th and 8th Infantry Divisions at Kabul, the 12th Infantry at Gardez, the 11th at Jalalabad, the 20th at Nahrin in Baghlan, the 19th at Herat, the 18th at Mazar-i-Sharif, the 9th at Chughai Serai in Balkh, the 15th at Khandahar, the 25th at Khost, and the 14th at Ghazni, with the 4th and 15th Armoured Divisions at

An Afghan RPG-7 gunner poses on the engine decking of his latest kill – a Soviet T-55 main battle tank

Kabul and the 7th Armoured at Kandahar; but the small and variable size of all Kabul regime units make such orders of battle a weak guide. Supplementing these forces are 18 000 police and 5000 militia. Several hundred East German advisors are reportedly re-organizing the Afghan police.

With these forces, what do the Soviets control? Simply, only as far as their direct fire weapons can reach. The countryside is firmly in the hands of the

(Right) These Afghans wear the light khaki uniforms of the Afghan Army and are fully armed with Soviet small arms and equipment. They are, however, fighting against the Soviets - part of one of many sub-units that have switched sides *en masse*

An Mi-8 helicopter is camouflaged after having defected to guerrilla forces. The 57 mm rockets have already been removed from the pods for use in improvised ground rocket launchers

Afghans, and even secure urban areas can be penetrated by Afghan attacks. Yet the balance of forces in Afghanistan will permit little else. The Soviets have encountered one of the largest popular risings of this century, the nearest comparison being that of Yugoslavia during the Second World War. Unless the Soviets were to commit massive forces at a great economic cost - forces that quite possibly could not be supplied without massive investments in logistic infrastructure such as building a railroad - they simply do not have enough people on the ground to occupy vital areas. Thus, the Soviets have apparently worked out a strategy that does not hinge on the occupation of territory, but rather on denying it to the Afghans.

Mao Tse-Tung wrote that the guerrilla must move among the people as a fish moves in the sea. The Soviets intend to drain the water. They attack the Afghan capability of operating in a particular area by removing the people there and destroying its agriculture, thus making the area unable to feed those who live there or any guerrillas.

The primary way of defeating the Afghans is by forcing them out of the country. Three and a half million Afghans are currently refugees, the largest single refugee population in the world, and one which is increasing daily. Air strikes by both fixed-wing aircraft

and Mi-24 *Hind* attack helicopters are used to force Afghans over the border. In addition to the air strikes, the Soviets leave their bases for sweep and cordon operations.

This is the Soviet Army's main form of offensive action in Afghanistan. It involves moving quickly to cordon off an area, particularly an agriculturally valuable one where Afghan guerrillas have been operating. The Soviets then move in, slowly, destroying granaries, flocks, and irrigation systems. Any civilians who survive being caught up in the cordon can then be re-settled in secure areas. Against the inexorable advance of Soviet units, the Afghans must avoid being drawn into a pitched battle where Soviet firepower – especially their helicopters – could be decisive. A month-long cordon-and-sweep operation of the Pansjir Valley began on August 20, 1981. By the time it was over, the Soviets had lost 30 armoured vehicles and five helicopters, but they had also inflicted heavy losses on the Afghans and destroyed much of the food that the Afghans needed to sustain them through the winter. Operations such as this shows what the future may bring in Afghanistan.

It is often said in the West that Afghanistan is the Soviet Union's Vietnam, but the view from Moscow and Kabul would surely show this to be an inapt analogy. It is true that the Soviets are faced with a country bigger than South Vietnam. They have but a third of the strength the Americans deployed in Vietnam. Where the Americans could count on Allied forces, the Soviets have none. The Soviet's erstwhile Afghan allies are thin on the ground and highly unreliable. Moreover, the terrain of Afghanistan is as hard for a modern army as was that of Vietnam. Yet with all these drawbacks, the Soviets are by no means as hard pressed as the Americans were in Vietnam. There are two reasons for this.

The first is that the internal government of the Soviet Union is much less vulnerable to the type of domestic and international political pressure that caused the United States to leave South-east Asia, or France to leave Algeria, or Portugal to leave Africa. Militarily, while the Afghans may win battles, they cannot defeat the full force of the Soviet Union on the battlefield. There is little chance of the Afghans being able to field and support a force that could defeat the Soviets. If the Afghans are to succeed, it must be by combining domestic and international pressure with continued resistance on the ground in Afghanistan. Until then, however, the Afghans remain short of everything except courage - a quality for which they have been known for over centuries, as have the Russian soldiers that they now fight.

The long struggle

The Afghans are currently a nation in arms. The Soviet invasion provoked guerrilla warfare throughout the country. Motivated by Islam, the different Afghan groups fight their own wars against the Soviets. While the 20th Century has invariably tended to over-romanticize the guerrilla, it remains that the Afghans have accomplished a great deal in action against the world's most powerful army.

Afghan strength is difficult to ascertain, as is the case with any guerrilla force. Some US government sources estimate that 90 000 Afghans are in the field at most times, while Afghans themselves claim 120 000 full-time cadres with a maximum of 250 000 in action at any one time. Other Afghan sources claim 300 000 under arms, but, as in any guerrilla war, it is the active or passive cooperation of the populace which is the guerrilla army's real strength, more than the actual numbers of fighting men.

Much has been made in the West about the factionalism and division among the Afghan groups. However, these divisions are inherent in the nature of Afghan society. A heterogenous collection of people divided by religion (Sunni, Shi'ite and Ismaili Moslems are all represented), language, ethnic groups, and tribes; once the validity of the Kabul regime was destroyed in the eyes of the Afghans, there was no centralizing authority to hold them together. While they all hold to the same religion and the same aim of

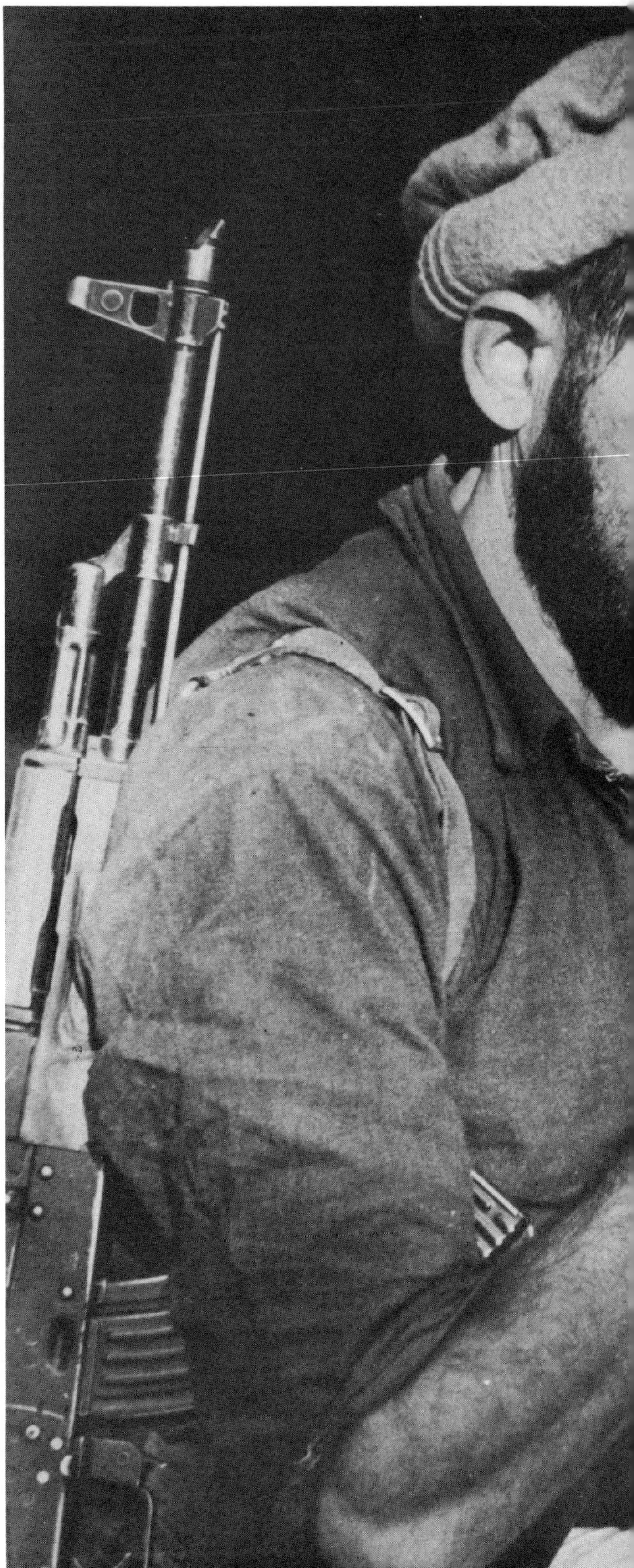

(Above) A display of Soviet munitions collected by Afghans

(Right) AK-47-armed Afghan at prayers. Islam is a prime unifying and motivating force in the Afghan resistance and many Afghans consider their struggle a *jihad*

defeating the Soviets, age-old animosities and Pathan blood feuds cannot always be put aside. Nevertheless, there is no constant, large-scale fighting between Afghan groups, despite published reports to the contrary.

The decentralized nature of the Afghan resistance is both a weakness and a strength. It makes it difficult (but by no means impossible) for the Afghans to coordinate large forces, but these in any case would be difficult to supply and would make good targets for air attacks. Indeed many different groups fought together successfully in the Khandahar fighting in the summer of 1981. Another benefit is that the Soviets cannot stem the lifeblood of the resistance by taking over its central headquarters or planning staff.

The level of resistance organization inside Afghanistan was originally at the local level, but by 1981, it had spread to the regional, with whole areas following a single leader in several parts of the country. Sometimes, these local or regional leaders are traditional tribal chiefs or Islamic *mullahs.* Others are charismatic guerrilla fighters thrust forward by battle. Those Afghans operating from Pakistan comprise a number of groups, which range the ideological spectrum from moderate pro-Western to strident Islamic fundamen-

talism. But whatever the philosophical gap between the leaders, it normally does not mean hostility between the fighting men in the field.

Weapons and tactics

There can seldom have ever been a more pronounced contrast in the weapons and tactics used by opposing combatants than in the Afghanistan War. The Soviets have fielded equipment that literally has no equal anywhere in the world – the T-72 tank with its reportedly ATGM-proof frontal 'combined armour', laser rangefinder and automatic loader and the *Hind-E* helicopter, able to use fire-and-forget AT-6 *Spiral* missiles. Soviet tactics have evolved through years of study and development. The basic Afghan weapon remains the bolt-action Lee-Enfield rifle, mainly locally produced copies of the Mk III. Afghan tactics are largely the brand of guerrilla warfare that the 'wily Pathan' has specialized in for centuries.

It says much for the old Indian Army that it was able, over the years, to get the measure of its opponents, Pathan and Afghan, without having the tremendous technological superiority the Soviets enjoy. Of course, much of this is due to the fact that the Raj never considered the effort needed to annex Afghanistan to be productive – one wonders whether a copy of Lord Roberts' *Kabul to Khandahar* passed around the Politburo in 1979 might have changed the course of events! Yet it also points out some fundamental inadequacies in Soviet tactics, which resulted in a number of defeats until they started to learn the lessons of the Indian Army.

Soviet tactics, intended to defeat NATO in Western Europe or the Chinese on the plains of Manchuria, were not easily adapted to this new style of warfare. Soviet motorized rifle and tank units were often road-bound, unable to come to grips with Afghans moving along the crests of hills with speed of experienced mountaineers. Low level tactics were particularly deficient, as was marksmanship. At long ranges, Soviet motorized riflemen, armed with Kalashnikovs and trained for automatic fire, are less liable to hit anything than Afghans behind *sangars* (rock breastworks) using Lee-Enfields and aimed fire. Nor were these the only failings. Tanks and armoured vehicles fell victim to improvised weapons and obstacles. Small convoys were overwhelmed in ambushes until the Soviets stopped running them. If the Soviets really thought, as some have suggested, that six or seven divisions could finish the job of ensuring that a regime hand-picked in Moscow would rule Afghanistan in a few months and then withdraw, they must have realized they were mistaken before 1980 was many months old.

The Soviets have continued to emphasize the use of

(Above left) A combat group of Afghans displays their wide variety of weaponry

(Above) Afghans line up for prayers and weapons inspection. Although this group is heavily armed with Soviet-made weapons, they are not carrying any captured gas masks, suggesting they are operating in an area where chemical weapons have not been used

(Left) These BTR-152s of the Afghan Army were knocked out in an ambush during fighting in Paktia province

their Afghan troops throughout these operations, despite their tendency to desert at any opportunity, taking their weapons with them, which have included T-54 tanks and, more importantly, mines, RPG-7 anti-tank rocket launchers and SA-7 man-portable surface-to-air-missiles. The Soviets relieved the Afghan Army of its inventory of man-portable anti-tank and air-defence weapons during 1980, and greatly reduced the scale of issue of all other supplies. Most of the Kabul regime's forces are infantry, which use comandeered trucks for mobility, making them more vulnerable to rifle fire than mechanized Soviet columns.

There is little doubt that the real cutting edge of the Soviet presence in Afghanistan is the helicopter. Helicopters provide the Soviets with both tactical mobility and mobile firepower. The *Hind* attack helicopter, 200 of which are in Afghanistan, has been particularly effective. Afghan leaders have stated that their most pressing need is for a weapon to combat these helicopters. As it is now, the heavily armoured *Hinds* can deliver their ordnance accurately and without much risk. The Soviets also seem to use *Hinds* for most of their close air-support missions. Mi-8 *Hip* helicopters, supplemented by larger Mi-6 *Hooks*, handle most of the troop-carrying and resupply missions.

The tactical benefits to the Soviets of their extensive

helicopter force are potentially decisive. Quick movement by helicopter allows the Soviets to cordon off areas before the Afghans can evacuate or reinforce. Helicopters bring supplies to positions where any convoy would have to fight its way through ambushes. Today, the Soviets use *Hinds* in a major convoy escort role. Adapting the old Indian Army tactics of 'cresting the heights' as the convoy moves along a road in the valley, *Hinds* will scout ahead of the convoy and then land troops to hold key positions until the convoy passes, while other *Hinds* are ready to support them in case of ambush. Once the convoy has passed, the troops are picked up and re-inserted further along the convoy route. The five Soviet air-assault brigades in Afghanistan work as the ground striking arm of the Soviet helicopter force.

The Soviets have, since 1979, introduced a number of weapons especially suited to Afghanistan conditions. The 30mm AGS-17 automatic grenade launcher has appeared in considerable numbers. The Soviets have found it an excellent source of firepower, both mounted and dismounted, and it is able to demolish Afghan *sangars*. Much use is being made of 5.45mm calibre assault rifles and light machine guns. The Afghans call the small calibre rounds the 'poison bullet' because few men hit by them survive. The plastic PFM-1 'butterfly' mine – based on the American 'dragontooth' of the 1960s – is surface dropped in tremendous numbers by helicopters. This greatly cuts down on Afghan mobility at night, when they conduct most of their operations.

Soviet tactics have also improved in many areas. *Hinds* adopted nap-of-the-earth type techniques in late 1980, apparently after some had been lost to SA-7s. In the Pansjir Valley offensive of 1981, Afghans reported that Soviet motorized rifle units were adopting new, more aggressive tactics. They were no longer sticking to the vehicles and the roads, but moving up along the ridges after the Afghans. The Soviets have learned from many of their earlier setbacks.

The Afghan's arsenal, in contrast, is insufficient to deal with the Soviets. In Wardak province, there are not even enough bolt-action rifles to go around, and *jezails*, the traditional Pathan long rifle, are still to be seen. Reports that arms from outside – especially from Egypt and other Islamic nations – have been reaching the Afghans have been largely overstated. The flow is little more than a trickle – due largely to the enormous pressure the Soviets have put upon the Pakistan government to clamp down on supplies to the Afghans,

Afghan medical care is minimal. Few of those seriously wounded far from hospitals in Pakistan or the few medical facilities inside Afghanistan survive

pressure which they underline by attacking Pakistani territory at regular intervals (although one flight of *Hind-As* in Afghan markings that shot up a Pakistani Army border post found an unpleasant surprise in the form of an M55 quad 0.50 machine gun mount, which the Pakistanis had emplaced for just such an occasion – it accounted for one of the *Hinds*).

What modern weapons the Afghans do have – and the numbers are increasing – have come chiefly from ralliers from the Afghan Army and those picked up on the battlefield. The presence of many Soviet-trained former Afghan Army members mean that the weapons can be skillfully employed, but the amount of hardware is still terribly low. The need for SA-7-type SAMs and anti-tank weapons is especially crucial now that the Soviets have restricted the use of them on their own side.

Afghan tactics follow classic guerrilla patterns – striking at lines of communication, avoiding pitched battles most of the time, although groups will unite and fight to seize an important objective or to defend a key area. Urban guerrillas carry the war to the streets of Kabul with their own tactics. The familiarity of many Afghans with Soviet tactics has definitely been an advantage, but none has apparently used this advantage better than Major Sayed Jaglan, leader of a force of Hazaras in Gazni province. He was an honour graduate of the Frunze Higher Military School in the Soviet Union and, in 1979-80, apparently would present the Soviets with situations that encouraged the application of a stereotyped 'school solution' – for which an ambush was already prepared.

Chemical warfare

One of the most important elements in the war has been the extensive use of chemical warfare by the Soviets. While the Soviets have repeatedly denied these accusations, and the voice of world opinion has yet to accuse them of such actions, the evidence is clear and convincing. (I have spoken personally to Afghans who have survived these attacks and to American-trained Afghan and Pakistani doctors who have treated chemical warfare victims and to Americans who have collected and analyzed samples. I regret to report that this is not an invention of the Washington propaganda mills. It is very real.)

The December 1979 invasion and the fighting following it included extensive use of a gas that appears to have been a concentrated type of CN – a normally non-lethal variety. But, soon afterwards, the Soviets apparently introduced tricothecene toxin (T-2), the 'yellow rain'. This agent is normally used in out-of-the-way localities and in areas where Soviet troops are not in contact. It is normally delivered by fixed-wing aircraft.

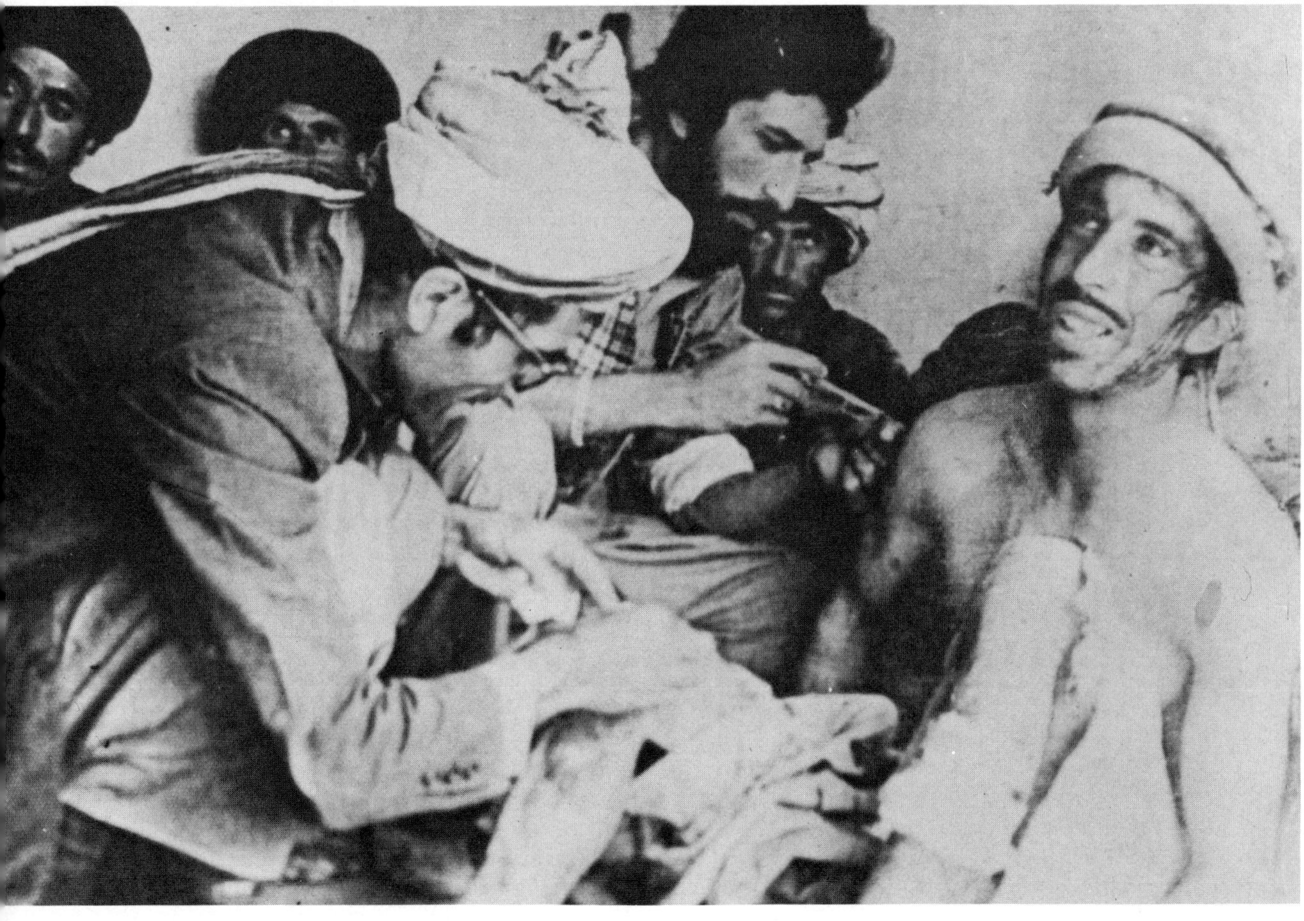

It is extremely toxic, and normally fatal within a brief amount of time.

The devastating effect of air strikes using this agent greatly contributes to the Soviet strategy of draining away the base of Afghan support, for nothing appears more likely to force people out of Afghanistan and into the refugee camps than chemical attacks. Evidence compiled by the US State Department shows that a minimum total of 47 attacks, causing 3042 deaths, can be reliably attributed to Soviet chemical warfare efforts in Afghanistan. Afghan sources believe the totals are much higher. For a strategy that must put a high premium on economy of force, as the Soviets currently do in Afghanistan, chemical weapons have a great value. Meanwhile, the use of incapacitating agents - and large amounts of standard nerve agents - continues in addition to the toxins.

Logistics

Logistics are, for both sides, one of the primary limitations on how they can wage their war. The basic Soviet strategy is, quite possibly, dictated to them by logistical considerations.

The Soviet Army has greatly improved its logistics system since the debacle of the 1968 invasion of Czechoslovakia. But the Soviet Army is still dependent on railroads for its primary operational-level supplies. As there are no railroads in Afghanistan, the Soviets must instead use large truck convoys moving down the Salang Pass highway from the Soviet Union to Kabul. Historically, truck convoys have been a difficult means of supplying whole armies, especially when they are limited to one or a few key roads. Rommel's difficulties in supplying *Panzerarmee Afrika* at Alamein with supplies being trucked along the *Via Balbia* from Tripoli are a prime example. Even the most effective truck convoy system - the US Army's 'Red Ball Express' of 1944 - burnt up resources at a tremendous rate. Given a long enough distance to move the supplies and large enough supply requirements, it is necessary to carry so much in fuel for the trucks, and supplies for the truck convoys and their escorts, that the end shipments reaching the combat troops will be relatively small (as happened to Rommel).

The Soviet strategy may well be dictated largely by the need to stockpile supplies for each operation. There is also some uncertainty over whether the Soviets could actually supply a force much larger than the one they have currently in Afghanistan simply because of the difficulties in sending more truck convoys (which would require even more fuel and even more escorts) down the main road from the Soviet Union.

Airlift can be a useful supplement for bringing in personnel and high-priority items, but with limited Soviet airlift resources and the need to bring in the fuel for returning transport aircraft, they cannot contribute substantially to the bottom line of tonnage requirements.

An Afghan Mi-8 *Hip*-C helicopter which came down in Paktia province in 1979

Afghan logistics are also difficult. They must draw their supplies from people in Afghanistan. But Afghan agriculture which, in different areas, is either dependent on irrigation or flocks (which require storehouses for winter fodder), is particularly vulnerable to attacks. It is much harder to feed Afghan fighting men than it was to feed the Viet Cong and North Vietnamese, whose logistic problems were tremendous. The Soviets realize this is the Afghan weakpoint, hence their policy of depopulating areas, driving peasants off the land and

destroying their agricultural capability.

While the main sources of Afghan weapons and ammunition supply have already been mentioned, these are supplemented by munitions hand-crafted by Pathan cottage industries in Pakistan, especially those centered around the town of Dherra. These produce weapons – including Kalashnikov copies – and ammunition. The Afghans, however, must pay for these in hard currency, which limits their use as a supply source. In addition, some of the groups in the north of Afghanistan have been seen to use considerable numbers of weapons of types produced in China, so there may be another, albeit limited, logistic line there.

War without end?

Any guerrilla war is merciless, but that in Afghanistan is particularly brutal. Both sides summarily butcher any prisoners. Afghan villagers have been massacred time and time again – both sides report this, but blame each other. While the figure estimated by some Afghans (of 1.5 million dead) is probably too high, it is a fact that Afghan losses have been very high, probably 500 000 to one million killed and wounded. The trek across the mountains to Pakistan where almost three million refugees now wait must have certainly claimed many thousands of lives. Except where there are Western-trained medical personnel, the Afghans have almost no medical support. Many of their wounded simply die for lack of treatment.

The Soviets cannot control the countryside of Afghanistan. Nor can they install a government in Kabul whose popularity will extend beyond the estimated 7000 Afghan communists. However, there are currently no apparent pressures, politically, militarily, or economically, that would force the Soviets to withdraw. The last Soviet military expansion into Asia ended with the withdrawal from North Iran in 1946 but this was the result of American pressure that amounted almost to an ultimatum. The Soviets have also withdrawn forces from Finland and Austria in the 1950s, in line with international agreements providing for the neutrality of those nations. But one thing that must weigh heavily against any Soviet withdrawal is the knowledge, which the events of 1978-79 brought home to the Soviets, that a Marxist regime cannot rule in Kabul without the Soviet Army being there to prop it up. If the Soviets leave, the Marxist regime will fall.

To the Soviets, a Marxist-Socialist regime is the highest currently attainable form of political development. It would contradict the iron laws of history to allow such a government, once established, to turn back to a non-Socialist form. It would mean that the Marxist Revolution was not irreversible – a hard thing for Party theoreticians to swallow. Even then, the Soviets may use the lives they have lost in Afghanistan as their justification for a continuous presence, just as Brezhnev invoked the memory of the Soviet soldiers killed liberating Czechoslovakia to justify the 1968 invasion.

Meanwhile, the Soviets seem to be profiting from their first real combat experience since 1945. There is evidence that the Soviets are sending officers to Afghanistan on six-month tours of duty, which would suggest that they desire as many as possible to have combat experience. This means that few officers will be in-country long enough to build up experience, leading to constant repetition of the same mistakes – a fact that plagued the US Army in Vietnam.

For all the success the Afghans have had, the weight of Soviet power must surely grind them down if they remain without support from outside. Unless the Soviets do withdraw – which is highly unlikely – the fighting will not stop, for the Afghans are not about to halt their resistance, even if it is reduced to the stage where only groups operating from inside Pakistan are still able to carry on the struggle. It will truly be a war without end. The realities of geopolitics are such that the Afghans are doing all in their power to force the Soviets to withdraw, but unless this power is increased, and linked to the leverage of the West, it is not likely to succeed. Otherwise, in the words of one Afghan leader 'all of us will die, and all that will be left is the soil of Afghanistan'.

Afghan air defence – the 12.7 DshK "Dushka" on a tripod mount is the standard air defence weapon. 14.5mm ZPU-1s and ZGU-1s are also used, as are a wide variety of improvised mounts. Some groups have 23mm ZU-23 guns. SA-7s remain few and far between

Air Power, the Falklands and the Future

John W.R. Taylor

In the seventy years that have elapsed since Britain created the Royal Flying Corps, made up of Military and Naval Wings, there has been endless controversy concerning the extent to which air forces should be subject to the dictates and demands of armies and navies.

Throughout most of the First World War, the primary duty of the air services of both sides was to perform reconnaissance missions for the armies on every front. Fighters were introduced to prevent the enemy's reconnaissance and artillery spotting aircraft from doing this work. Other fighters were then needed to escort the reconnaissance aircraft and protect them from interception. Bombers had an initial major task of attacking the airfields from which the other side's fighter and reconnaissance aircraft - including Zeppelin airships-operated. What we now term ground attack, strategic bombing and other military aviation roles became increasingly important; but the key importance of reconnaissance and intelligence has never changed.

Within four years of that war's ending, Brig Gen 'Billy' Mitchell of the US Air Service demonstrated the capability of the heavy bombers of the time, to his own satisfaction, by using them to sink three old German battleships and two obsolete US battleships off the American coastline. The US Navy countered by suggesting that the outcome might have been different had the ships been mobile, manned and able to hit back. Mitchell was eventually court-martialled and suspended from duty.

Sixteen years later, the United States were again involved in a world war, which began for them when the

Short Belfast of Heavy lift freight airlines - sold out of RAF service in 1976 and hurriedly requisitioned to join the Falklands airlift to Ascension Island

Japanese directed a crippling air attack on their fleet at Pearl Harbor. Within three days, the two most powerful ships in the Royal Navy's Far Eastern Fleet had been sunk by Japanese torpedo-bombers when they sailed beyond the range of protective air cover. In this present year of 1982, other ships of a Royal Navy task force suffered similarly when they ventured within reach of enemy air power without airborne early warning aircraft to alert their crews when attacks were on the way. Yet, it is suggested officially that the campaign in the Falkland Islands was too recent to inspire any immediate rethinking of defence policy.

During the Second World War, the German Luftwaffe fought with aircraft intended mainly for army support. It smashed a path for armies that occupied much of continental Europe in 1940-41. But the Luftwaffe lacked the right aircraft, or the right directive, to win the Battle of Britain, and it proved quite incapable of halting the subsequent massive Allied bomber offensive against its homeland. Debate on the effectiveness of that bombing has never ceased, but no-one disputes that the war ended within days of the dropping of just two atomic bombs on Japanese cities.

So impressed were politicians with the terrible destructive power of the new weapons that a deterrent policy of 'peace through fear of nuclear annihilation' was adopted as the cornerstone of Western defence, matched far more quickly than had been anticipated by comparable weapons and thought on the other side of the barrier that had appeared across central Europe.

Britain's Conservative Defence Minister, Duncan Sandys, went further in 1957. In the government's annual *White Paper* on Defence he stated that such good progress was being made in the development of surface-

Harrier GR 1s, Britain's unique combat aircraft

to-air missiles, ballistic rockets and missile defence that it had been decided to abandon costly plans for further fighter aircraft or bombers beyond the Lightning, Vulcan and Victor then in production. Except for a modest number of strategic nuclear missiles, it was intended that Britain's three armed services should eventually become purely tactical and interdependent, seldom straying operationally beyond the European boundaries of NATO.

Britain's continuing possession of nuclear missiles did not deter occupation of the Falkland Islands by Argentina in 1982. Nor, it seems, did the Argentine leaders feel at any great disadvantage during the subsequent campaign because they had no nuclear weapons. In fact, like the Americans in Korea thirty years earlier, the British naval, air and land forces found themselves subjected to air attack, in what they believed to be British sovereign territory, by aircraft operating from mainland bases which had been ruled 'out of bounds' for counter-attack.

Clearly, it is time that somebody in authority began learning lessons, not solely from the Falklands

campaign but from all the evidence of 37 years of wrong decisions.

The Royal Navy task force had to ensure the safe passage of the land force to a combat area 8,000 miles from home, and protect it on arrival. It was led by one aircraft carrier that had been serving out its time before being scrapped, and another that was about to be sold to Australia. The only aircraft capable of hauling really heavy equipment to the nearest available base, on Ascension Island, were ex-RAF Short Belfasts that had been taken out of service to save money, and had been saved from the scrapyard by the private operator in whose colours they flew. The Harriers and Sea Harriers that were to provide such outstanding service in air attack and defence came from an RAF/Royal Navy inventory totalling fewer than 100 aircraft, many forming an indispensable part of NATO's first-line defences in Europe. The first of them had been bought reluctantly as lower-cost substitutes for more advanced aircraft that were considered too expensive by Harold Wilson's Labour government in the mid-sixties.

Despite the 1957 Sandys *White Paper*, the defence staff had managed to put some things right by the early sixties. Recognising that front-line airfields would be primary targets for elimination in the opening minutes of any future war, leaving NATO troops at the mercy of aircraft drawn from the 4,350 combat aircraft/helicopter strength of Soviet Frontal Aviation air armies, Britain's aircraft industry had devised a family of aircraft that could dispense with long paved runways. The Hawker P.1154 was intended to be a supersonic successor to the vertical take-off P.1127 Kestrel, of which it was planned to buy no more than the nine equipping a NATO three-nation evaluation squadron. The Hawker Siddeley 681 was under development as a tactical jet transport able to operate into and from small airstrips in combat areas. As well as ferrying in ground crews, munitions, fuel and supplies needed to keep the P.1154s in action, it was designed to carry the majority of current and projected British army vehicles and equipment, and to fill troop carrying, casualty evacuation and paratroop dropping roles.

In company with the TSR.2 supersonic bomber, that had fought its way into the air despite the sniping of successive governments, the P.1154 and HS 681 were abandoned in a now-familiar cost-cutting programme. Britain was not alone in this. On the other side of the Atlantic, some years later, a pair of revolutionary advanced Medium STOL (short take-off and landing) transports which had proved capable of carrying huge loads into and out of small airfields, failed to progress beyond the prototype stage. To save money, two types that had begun life as experimental low-cost lightweight fighters were ordered into massive production, to provide numerical support for the more traditional and very expensive F-14 Tomcat and F-15 Eagle. By the time they have been fully equipped, by retrospective

The B-1B destined to carry forward the manned bomber component of the US strategic triad

Dassault Super Etendard armed with the AM 39 Exocet – the Royal Navy's deadliest adversary in the South Atlantic

modification, they are expected to cost more than the F-14 and F-15.

While billions of pounds, dollars and roubles continued to be poured into gaping missile silos and missile-launching submarines, the United States first cancelled, and then re-ordered, the mighty B-1 bomber. The US Navy continued putting larger aircraft carriers into service, seemingly deaf to the advice of one of its former senior admirals, who had experienced many moments of frustration when narrow seas, or inconvenient winds, made it impossible to fly off his conventional heavy supersonic fighters. 'What your Royal Navy wants,' he told the writer, 'is a whole fleet of small, 10,000-ton Harrier carriers.' What it expected to get were three sister ships of nearly twice that displacement, one of which within weeks of its launch by the Queen Mother, was stated to be destined for mothballing, while another was to be sold to the Royal Australian Navy. The Sea Harriers that these ships carry were ordered despite a decision that the Fleet Air Arm would never again operate fixed-wing aircraft, only helicopters. Because of that same decision, and in the interests of money-saving, the Falklands task force sailed south without airborne early warning aircraft like the Gannets which once provided a radar screen for old-fashioned carriers.

The Royal Navy, like Britain's other armed forces, is tailored tightly to its NATO role, where it can expect to be screened by USAF/NATO E-3A Sentry airborne early warning and fighter control system (AWACS) aircraft, and US Navy Carrier-borne Hawkeyes. Off the Falklands, its destroyers had to provide radar picket

cover, and paid the price. As long ago as 1969 a Foreword in *Jane's All the World's Aircraft* commented: 'The Exocet missile . . . is designed to race towards its target at high subsonic speed, in all weathers, a mere six to ten feet above the water, over a range of more than 20 miles, in an ECM environment. How can one possibly defend a ship against such a missile?' The current edition states that the Argentine Navy ordered 14 Super Etendard attack aircraft from France in 1979. An illustration on the same page shows a Super Etendard taking off with an Exocet anti-ship missile under its wing. Adding two and two correctly can sometimes shape history.

C.G. Grey, second of four editors of *All the World's*

Argentinian Pucara – designed to combat guerrilla insurgents – pitched into action against a first division modern air defence

Aircraft, wrote: 'History is the greatest plagiarist in all literature, and repeats itself to such an extent that if one knew all history one would never make a mistake in life, because one would know of all the mistakes which can be made . . . However, those who would rather learn from bitter experience than from history need not read this stuff.'

For anyone willing to learn, both the lessons and possible remedies are discernible, and could minimise casualties if the Navy ever again has to carry and support an army in action. Nor need the remedies drain any nation's economy if the present immense international overkill, represented by the 3,976 intercontinental and submarine-launched ballistic missiles (ICBMs/SLBMs) in the hands of the USA and Soviet Union, is trimmed to the far smaller number necessary to remove each other's nation and peoples effectively from the map for all time – and if Britain accepts that its own added SLBM deterrent no longer deters anyone.

The Falklands affair may go down in history as just another limited campaign, of little significance to the world at large; but it was of supreme importance to the families of those who died, on both sides. *Jane's* is international and non-political; but it does seem, in this relatively enlightened age, that the people of any land should be entitled to choose the kind of government under which they wish to live, equally free from threats of aggression or of neglect until the threats are carried out. President Reagan, in choosing to support Britain, pointed out that he really had no choice because there are around 50 other places in the world where the same thing could happen if nobody had the courage to oppose it.

At this stage, one must ask why nations can still be taken by surprise as, apparently, Israel was at the start of the 1973 war with Egypt, and Britain was when the Argentine force began to go ashore at Port Stanley. Should not reconnaissance satellites help to preserve the peace for all nations, rather than for only the two so-called super-powers?

Assuming that this will not happen, and that the United Nations will continue to have no teeth, how can trouble be contained if it erupts in any of those other 50 places to which President Reagan referred? The easiest way to answer this question is to superimpose optimum equipment and capability into the scenario of the Falklands campaign, while recognising that its remoteness and extreme climatic conditions might have been unique. So were some of the factors that restricted casualties on both sides, such as the long tradition of friendship between the British and Argentine peoples; reluctance to shed blood needlessly on both sides, and to counter-attack mainland air bases even after heavy naval losses; and the inherent differences between a largely conscript army and an elite professional force made up of Paratroops, Commandos, Special Air Service, Special Boat Service, Guards and Gurkhas.

The first task should have been to eliminate completely the air bases on the Falklands. This was no task for geriatric super-stars like the Vulcans, needing several in-flight refuellings en route, and carrying 1,000 lb bombs for use against runways of solid rock with a thin paved skin. Some of the thousands of millions of pounds that would be saved by abandoning

(Right) Typical of the growing sophistication of conventional air landed munitions this is an MBB proposal for a modular stand off weapon capable of delivering a range of sub-munitions against the area targeted

(Below) Boeing E-3A AWACS now operational, providing a highly sophisticated early warning and fighter control system for NATO – but how long would they last in actual combat when they would be primary targets for every air power?

the useless British Trident submarine programme could be spent on buying two squadrons of B-1B bombers, able to carry the kind of runway-destroying munitions, and airfield-closing scatter weapons for which European companies like MBB and Hunting have well-deserved reputations.

Having cleared the immediate combat area of enemy air opposition, the next step would be to ensure that no surprise attack on the ships or troops ashore could be mounted from mainland bases. This calls for some form of AWACS; but aircraft like the E-3A, Hawkeye, and Nimrod AEW.3 have yet to prove themselves survivable beyond the opening minutes of any future conflict. Clearly, they would be primary targets for any aggressor who hoped to achieve any measure of surprise in attack or freedom from interception.

However much ECM equipment such an aircraft carries, the fact that it is of use only when it transmits data to its own side makes it easier to locate. Its onboard equipment would warn it of any approaching threat, and it could carry air-to-air missiles on a reloadable launcher; but would this be adequate? A better solution might be some form of long-endurance unmanned AWACS RPV (remotely piloted vehicle), on the lines of the Compass Copes built and tested by Boeing and Teledyne Ryan in the USA in the early seventies, which could remain airborne at great heights for periods of well over 24 hours. Made of glassfibre, they offered minimal radar signatures, and it may be significant that such a vehicle, on a small scale, is under test by NASA, though not with obvious military application at present.

Knowing in good time that an attack force was on the way, and from which precise direction, would enable the task force ships, and troops ashore, to prepare their missiles for action and deploy their interceptors. Impressive successes achieved against great odds by anti-aircraft missile operators and Harrier pilots in the Falklands suggest that the attackers would then face a very rough reception indeed.

The mix of V/STOL combat aircraft and helicopters available to the Royal Air Force and Royal Navy, almost by accident, was the only form of air power that could have played an effective part in such a campaign, being independent of prepared runways. It is no coincidence

(Below) A C-5A Galaxy unloads an SH-60 Blackhawk helicopter of the US Army 101st Airborne Division. The USAF possess massive airlift capacity but not enough to satisfy the needs of replenishing NATO in Europe in time of war

(Right) The A-10 Thunderbolt II, began life as a cheap and rugged tank-busting machine, but demands for additional weapons and sensors threaten to make it expensive and delicate

that the US Marine Corps intends to re-equip its attack units with advanced AV-8B Harrier IIs before the end of the decade. But how well could NATO cope with a major war in Europe?

The essential build-up would be so intense that NATO expects three or four weeks' warning, enabling it to reinforce greatly the air and land forces in Europe. This time there would be no shortage of information from satellites and AWACS aircraft, although the ability of the Soviet Union to destroy orbiting satellites is acknowledged. A major problem is that USAF's current force of 77 C-5 Galaxy heavy transports would be able to haul less than 50 per cent of all the outsize cargo needed in the first 20 days of a conflict. Needing to provide for an additional 25 million ton-miles of cargo per day, USAF requested 50 new C-5s, having already been refused the more advanced, all-new, STOL C-17s that it wanted. It was told to look instead into the possibility of buying second-hand Boeing 747s from airlines with financial problems.

Once the armies had taken up their forward positions in Europe, they would expect to be well supported by the large and efficient air forces deployed by NATO. Again there are snags. If the Warsaw Pact air forces mounted an attack on a dark night, or in thoroughly nasty weather of the kind that is all too common in Europe, this would make life difficult for the pilots of a high proportion of NATO's fighter and attack squadrons, whose aircraft are not completely equipped for all-weather operation. Fitting radar and other all-weather equipment to types like the A-10 Thunderbolt II close support aircraft can be done but costs money. The electro-optical guidance systems of missiles like the air-to-surface Maverick are also better suited to sunny California than Germany.

Deadly Ground Fire

Bearing in mind that the spearhead of an assault, after

an initial softening up by artillery and aircraft, might be a force of several hundred troop-carrying and heavily armed helicopters, there is a clear need for defensive aircraft able to deal with such a threat. No-one has yet built a single-seat helicopter fighter, but Harriers could probably do the job if there were enough of them. This would demand very careful designation of aircraft/ground-fire killing zones, and simple efficient IFF (identification, friend or foe), or the NATO troops would probably shoot down an equal mix of enemy and friendly aircraft. Experience in Vietnam, the Middle East and the Falklands leaves little doubt of how deadly missiles like the SAM-7 and Blowpipe can be against low-flying aircraft.

B-1B bombers, Harriers, fighter helicopters, AWACS RPVs, surface-to-air missiles, all-weather equipment, heavy-lift transports . . . the cost of putting an army where it needs to be, and then supporting it, becomes alarming. There are alternatives. One is to live in peace under the worldwide protection of a UN multinational force, adequately equipped with weapons of every kind (including a handful of SLBMs) needed to deter even a super-power. Another is to acknowledge that conventional weapons are too costly, and be prepared to drop neutron bombs, or push the first button at an ICBM silo, or on board an SLBM-carrying submarine in the first seconds of an attack. However, nobody has yet worked out a way of coping with 250 million corpses on three continents, or how those unfortunate enough to survive would manage with no safe food to eat or water to drink, no fuels to move and warm them, or electricity, or telephones, or radio, or television – or hope.

An American AH-64 Apache helicopter carrying a profusion of sophisticated weapons and sensing devices

The Soviet SA-7 SAM is widely distributed throughout the world and is a good example of the potent air-defence weapons now available to ground troops

Pictures from an Exhibition

The British Army Equipment Exhibition, 1982

The biennial British Army Equipment Exhibition takes place in two venues: the static exhibition at Aldershot, and the Mobility and Firepower demonstrations at Bovingdon. The 1982 displays brought some new equipment to the public's eye and also gave a useful reminder of the abilities of some older items. An innovation this year was the inclusion of an aquatic display area at Hawley Lake, which allowed bridging and ferrying equipment to be seen in a realistic setting for the first time.

(Left below) One of the stars of the show was the new Chieftain 900 tank, developed as a private venture by the Royal Ordnance Factories organisation with a view to the export market

(Left) The Royal Ordnance Factories stand displayed all their latest products, including this turret with 120mm gun

(Below) A last-minute surprise was this 'Simba' armoured vehicle from GKN-Sankey, complete with Cockerill 90mm gun. It is believed that substantial orders have already been received from the Middle East

(Bottom) Vickers Shipbuilding & Engineering were showing their new GBT-155 turret, and also displayed it, shown here, mounted on the well-known Vickers Mark III tank chassis so as to provide a useful and cost-effective self-propelled artillery equipment

Blowpipe
TOW

(Far left) The Tripartite SP-70 155mm SP howitzer programme is slowly approaching completion; this is the latest in a long series of prototype models and appears to be a cleaner design than some of its forebears

(Left below) The Hawley Lake display area showed the Army in some unfamiliar postures. Here are RCT soldiers manning workboats and floating ferries

(Below) Vickers have also developed a simple but effective ammunition hoist and loading aid for use with the FH-70 howitzer. Relying upon spring power to balance the shell's weight, it eases the work of the loaders

(Left) The Townley Six, one of several six-wheel variations of the Land Rover, mounting a twin launcher for the Blowpipe missile system

04 BT 66

08 SP 39

(Below left) Star of the show was the new Challenger main battle tank, seen going through its paces in public for the first time

(Below) The firing display included units of the Royal Artillery, firing 105mm and 155mm weapons; this is the FH-70 demonstrating the smoke pattern from its muzzle brake

(Far left) The 'Saboteur' all-terrain vehicle, carrying a Milan anti-tank missile

(Left) The Chieftain 900 demonstrates its ability to track a target while surmounting some of the rougher parts of the cross-country course

(Below) The Combat Engineer Tractor towing a Giant Viper mine-clearing device

(Far left) GKN-Sankey's new MCV-80 takes the cross-country obstacles in its stride

(Left) The Alvis Scorpion 90 attracted a great deal of attention both at Aldershot and Bovingdon

(Bottom) The more utilitarian side of military life is not neglected, as this new tank transporter showed

Optronics

Charles Castle

Optronics is a new-coined word constructed from 'optics' and 'electronics', and it is a word which will be heard more and more in future. In the middle 1930s the principal concern of defence scientists was the detection of aircraft at long ranges, and the two physical characteristics of the aeroplane which looked as if they could be utilised were engine noise and engine heat. Sound detection had been in use for years, and so research was directed to the use of infra-red techniques to detect engine heat. Radar was in its infancy and promised well, but infra-red detection equipment, if it could be carried in an aircraft, might be of use in night-fighters to 'close the gap' between ground intercept radar and the pilot's own eyesight. Some of the early story is to be found in Professor R.V. Jones' 'Most Secret War'. Infra-red was eventually abandoned for aircraft detection, but it was revived later in the war as a driving aid for vehicle drivers and as a sighting aid for snipers. In this latter role the Americans developed the 'Sniperscope', which consisted of a large infra-red searchlight mounted above a .30 carbine, and an infra-red sensitive telescopic sight. It had its drawbacks; it was heavy and cumbersome and it demanded a heavy pack of batteries which had to be carried by the sniper, but it worked over short ranges, bathing the target in an eery green light which allowed an accurate shot to be made at ranges up to about 200 metres in pitch darkness.

The possibility of using infra-red had occurred to several inventors before the war, and a number of patents were taken out by private individuals, so many in fact that German technical observers came to the conclusion that the British forces must be pushing infra-red at a powerful rate; they therefore began development of their own and during the course of the war surpassed most other people in the range and efficiency of their equipment.

Infra-red, as it stood in 1945, had one prime defect; it generally required the use of an infra-red light source, and this meant that the operator was putting out a detectable signal which could be picked up by a relatively simple piece of equipment at ranges beyond those at which he could see a target. For this reason

(Left) A British sentry in Norway, with a first-generation 'Night Observation Device' and (right) a laser rangefinder at his disposal

(Below) The Pilkington 'Pocketscope' second-generation hand-held viewer, easily portable and of great value to night infantry patrols

most of the apparatus developed during the war was dropped and research was concentrated into 'passive' infra-red, simply detecting the heat emitted by the target; this, of course, was what had started it all off, and it was the system which the Germans had developed with considerable success, notably in various coast-watching equipment which could detect ships at sea some 15 km away from shore.

'Research moved slowly, however, and it was not until the Americans became involved in the Vietnam war that there was much incentive; the US Army then began demanding something in the order of the 'Sniperscope'. Their demand more or less coincided with the development of miniaturised electronic circuitry, lightweight batteries and several other scientific innovations and the result led to the first steps into electro-optics or optronics.

The innovation was the 'image intensifying sight' which gave results far better than the old-time Sniperscope and did it with far less equipment. The technique evolved was to focus the visible image - such as it was - on to a photo-sensitive screen. This would emit electrons on its inner side in proportion to the light which fell on it from the lens. These electrons could then be amplified, by fairly conventional electronic techniques, and projected onto another screen which would glow in response to the electrons striking it. This screen could now be viewed by a conventional optical eyepiece and the viewer saw something resembling a small television picture. What had happened was that the very slight differences in contrast of the scene had been artificially accentuated by the electronic amplification. Instead of the difference between light and dark parts of the scene being as, say, 2:1 they now become as 50:1 and so a dim star- or moonlit-scene was now as distinct as if being viewed by noonday sunlight.

In fact the single stage of amplification gave a gain of about 4000×, and although this sounds enormous it was not really good enough. So the amplified electron stream was made to impinge upon another emitting screen; the electrons from this were amplified and projected onto a third screen, and the electrons from this were amplified and projected on to the viewing screen. There were thus three stages of amplification giving a gain of about 64,000×, and this system gave rise to the term 'cascade tube' to describe the three-stage instrument.

The result in practice was a telescope-like device, usually about 400 mm long, which could be mounted on top of a rifle or machine gun in much the same way as a conventional optical sight and, indeed, be used in much the same way as well. The operator switched it on, looked through it, saw the amplified scene with an aiming crosswire, and fired. The range varied according to the light-gathering ability of the prime lens and the quality of the electronics, but was usually about 300 m

(Right) An image-intensifying sight mounted on a silenced submachine-gun

(Above) The Pilkington 'Snipe' second-generation rifle sight

in starlight, 400 m in moonlight against a man-sized target. Similar instruments were also provided for hand-held viewing of an area, for use on reconnaissance patrols.

The virtues of this image-intensifying sight were soon apparent to the soldiers who began demanding more range, better definition, less weight and various other improvements. The first response was to develop larger and heavier models which improved range and definition, and these became surveillance instruments for artillery and infantry observation posts. These pushed the range at which a man could be detected out to 1200-1500 metres, and at greater ranges than this they could detect large objects such as tanks and trucks and give a good impression of the countryside for five or six kilometres.

But the search for lighter sights made little progress until a completely new type of intensifier was developed. This was the 'micro-channel amplifier', a device consisting of a bundle of extremely fine fibres - several million of them in a tube some 18 mm in diameter. A receptor screen at the front end receives the

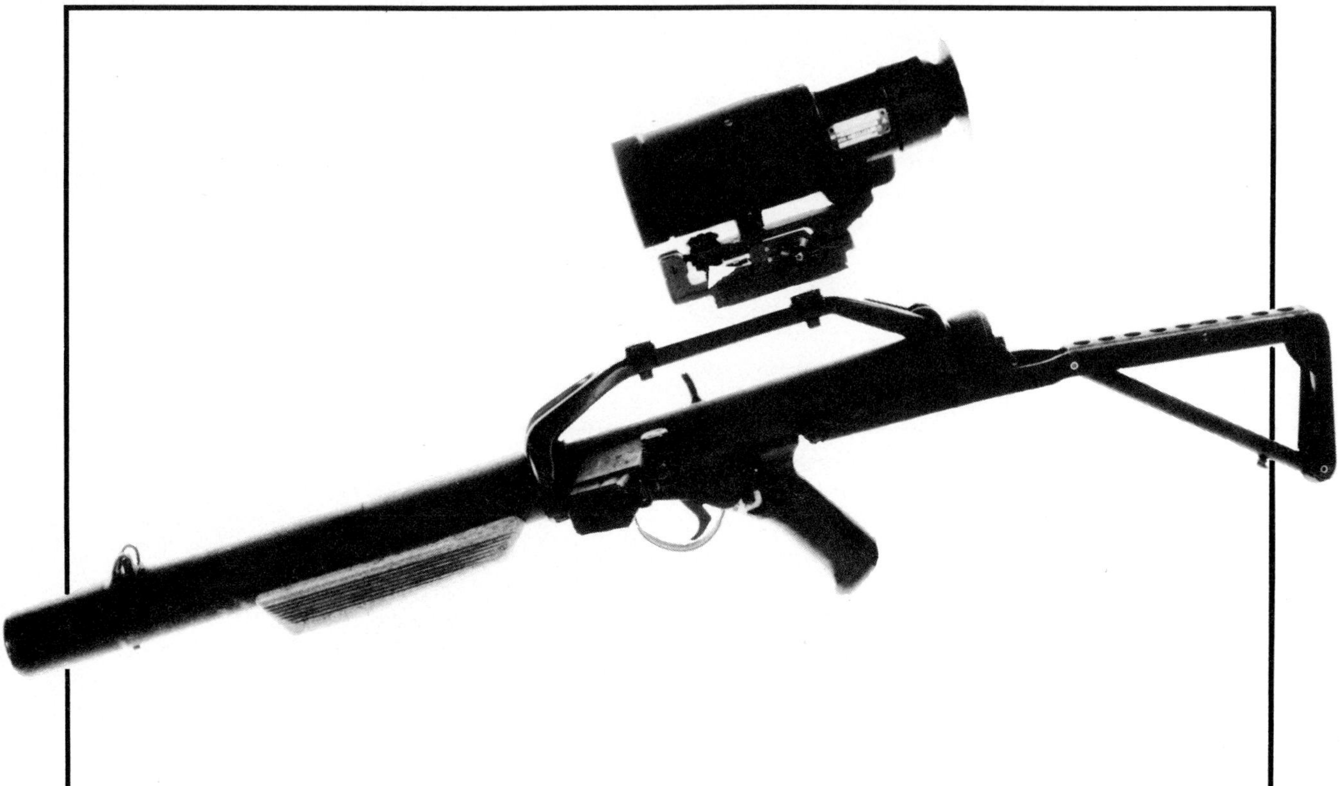

optical image and generates electrons which are fed into the micro-channels. The amplifier unit is fed by an electrical field and in their progress down the channels the electrons 'ricochet' from the sides and generate additional electrons, so that the signal coming out of the channel is much greater than that which went in. The outgoing electrons impinge on another screen and provide a visual image; this can either be viewed by an eyepiece or given further amplification by another micro-channel amplifier.

The micro-channel amplifier is much more compact than the original pattern and a single unit gives a much greater degree of amplification; nothing, however, is for nothing, and this 'second-generation' device is much more expensive than the 'first-generation' cascade tube device, both by virtue of its complexity and also because there is a high rejection rate during manufacture. Nevertheless, a second generation image intensifier can be much more compact, for a given degree of amplification, than a first generation unit, so that sights and observation devices can be much smaller and lighter. In fact they can be so light that it is now possible to develop a binocular viewer, using a single micro-channel amplifier, which can be worn like an over-sized pair of spectacles, leaving the user's hands free. Thus it can be worn as a night vision aid by vehicle drivers and helicopter pilots, or even by a platoon commander for reading a map in the dark.

Second generation devices are in widespread use by military forces in several armies, and the scientists are now looking to the 'third generation'. This is to be achieved by using the same micro-channel amplifier but treating the receiving and viewing screens with improved phosphors so that more electrons are generated by the light which strikes and a brighter picture is generated by the emitted electrons at the other end of the amplifier. The instruments may not be very much smaller, but their amplification will certainly be better and the displayed picture will also be of higher quality. It is generally expected that third generation instruments will become fit for military service by about 1984.

Whilst image intensification is highly effective, the fact remains that there must be *some* light before they can function, since they rely solely upon amplifying what little light there is. In pitch darkness they cannot work at all. To cater for this, the thermal imager has been developed and has now reached a degree of perfection at which it is competing with image intensification for service use.

'Thermal imaging' is the current phrase for passive infra-red; it relies upon detecting the heat differences in the viewed area, and it can discern quite minute temperature changes, as little as half a degree Centigrade, at quite long ranges. The area of search is rapidly scanned in a pattern of lines similar to that seen on a television tube and relayed to a sensitive grid which

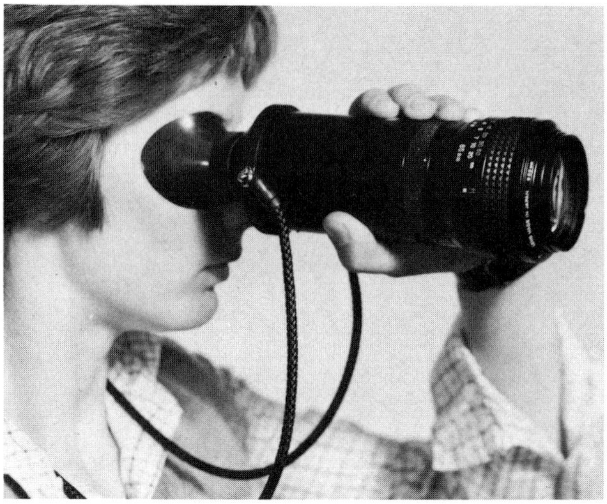

(Below) A range of optronic night vision equipment from the Italian company Officine Galileo, including sights for infantry weapons and tank guns

(Right) A helicopter pilot wearing image intensifying goggles to permit him to identify targets at night

(Above) An example of a lightweight hand-held image intensifying viewer for use by civil security forces

builds up a picture in which the hotter parts of the scene are distinguished from the cooler parts. By simple adjustment of polarity, hot can be represented by white or by black, as the viewer chooses, and the resulting picture is then viewed by an optical eyepiece. Since the picture is built up electronically it is possible to arrange the linearity of the scan to match current television standards and so transmit the picture by television techniques, either by cable or by radio, to a distant viewer. Thus, for instance, it is possible to place a scanner in the head of a submarine periscope and transmit the results by cable to a viewer in the submarine control room, a system which gives a far more efficient result than attempting to transfer the image by optical methods.

Thermal imaging devices require power, and some require cooling systems to work at their optimum efficiency, and therefore they are best employed in circumstances where such adjuncts are easily provided. They are, as a result, often to be seen in tank driving and sighting devices and as surveillance instruments; their use as portable weapon sights is less common.

An Italian company, Officine Galileo, have made an ingenious attempt to produce a weapon sight giving the best of both worlds, a sight which combines both thermal imaging and image intensification in the same unit. The operator can select either system or both at once; thermal imaging gives advantages of range – it can detect a warm target at greater distances than the image intensifier can pick them out – and it can also, to some extent, defeat camouflage since it senses the heat of the concealed object through the visual screen. Image intensification, on the other hand, gives better resolution and definition once the target is in range, so that the operator can use the TI unit for 'early warning' and then switch to II for close range operation. Both can be used together, giving an infra-red detecting 'overlay' to the image intensifier picture, so allowing, for example, camouflaged targets to be detected and engaged.

In the face of all this technology the soldier requires some guidance, for this is a field in which the simple adage 'this is new, therefore it is good' is not necessarily true. The first generation image intensifier, for example, gives a better performance in very low light levels than does the second generation, so that there are technical, as well as economic, reasons for retaining these instruments in service. Against that, the first generation instrument emits a distinctive high-pitched whine during operation; this is almost inaudible to the human ear but has been found to upset animals, and their reaction has been known to compromise an otherwise well-concealed observer. In recent months there has been activity in the development of pyrotechnic smokes which have been 'doped' so as to inhibit infra-red vision; these have been primarily developed as a means of defending armoured vehicles from IR-guided anti-tank missiles, but they will also make life extremely difficult for vision devices, since, of course, the smoke will prevent observation by image intensifiers even without the added refinement of stopping thermal imagers.

Night vision techniques also have a great deal of civil applications – thermal imaging can be used in airports to 'see through' the glare of runway lights and make a visual check of aircraft coming in to land, to see, for example, that the undercarriage is down and the flaps correctly deployed; it has wide applications in security, checking the integrity of factory surroundings, keeping watch inside empty and dark buildings; the principle can even be used in medicine to scan the human body and detect 'hot spots' indicative of disease. Image intensifiers are also in use by security companies as surveillance devices, either as hand-held viewers or in conjunction with closed-circuit television cameras, relaying pictures back to a central control room.

The recent activities in the Falkland Islands have seen several instances of the use of night vision devices, both by the British troops and by the Argentines. So far as the soldier is concerned, night has been turned into

(Right) The American AN/TAS-6 Night Observation Device, Long Range, mounted on a tripod

(Below) A Thermal-imaging camera unit mounted in the nose of a French helicopter to permit firing HOT anti-tank missiles at night

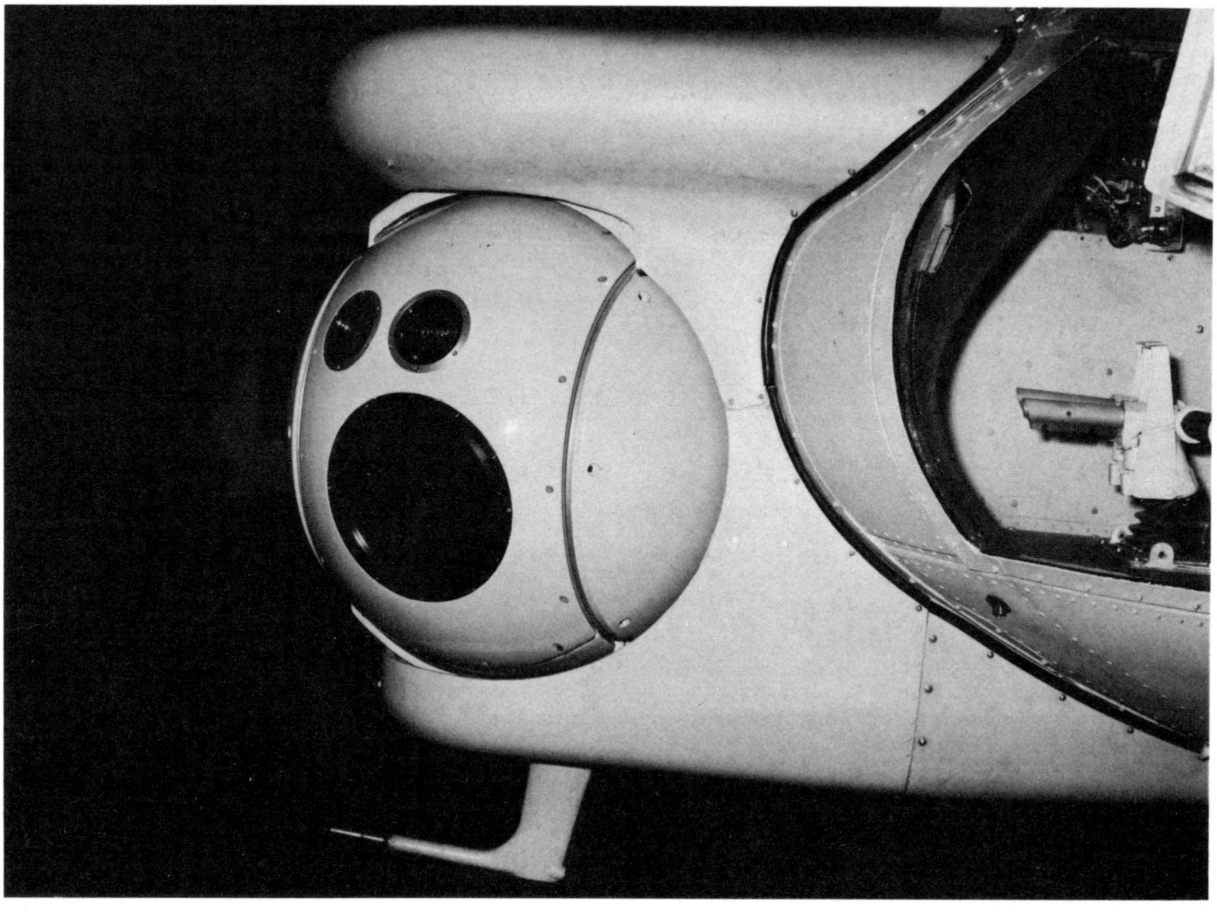

day, but the advantages of this are somewhat mixed. In years gone by, night was the time the troops snatched some rest, fairly secure from interference; this is no longer the case, since tactical operations can be conducted as easily at night as they are by day, and the implications of this on the battlefield have yet to be fully examined. Troops operating by day and resting by night have an endurance which is, by now, fairly well calculable; troops asked to operate 24 hours per day will have far less endurance, and the effect of this on future operations is something which will require close study.

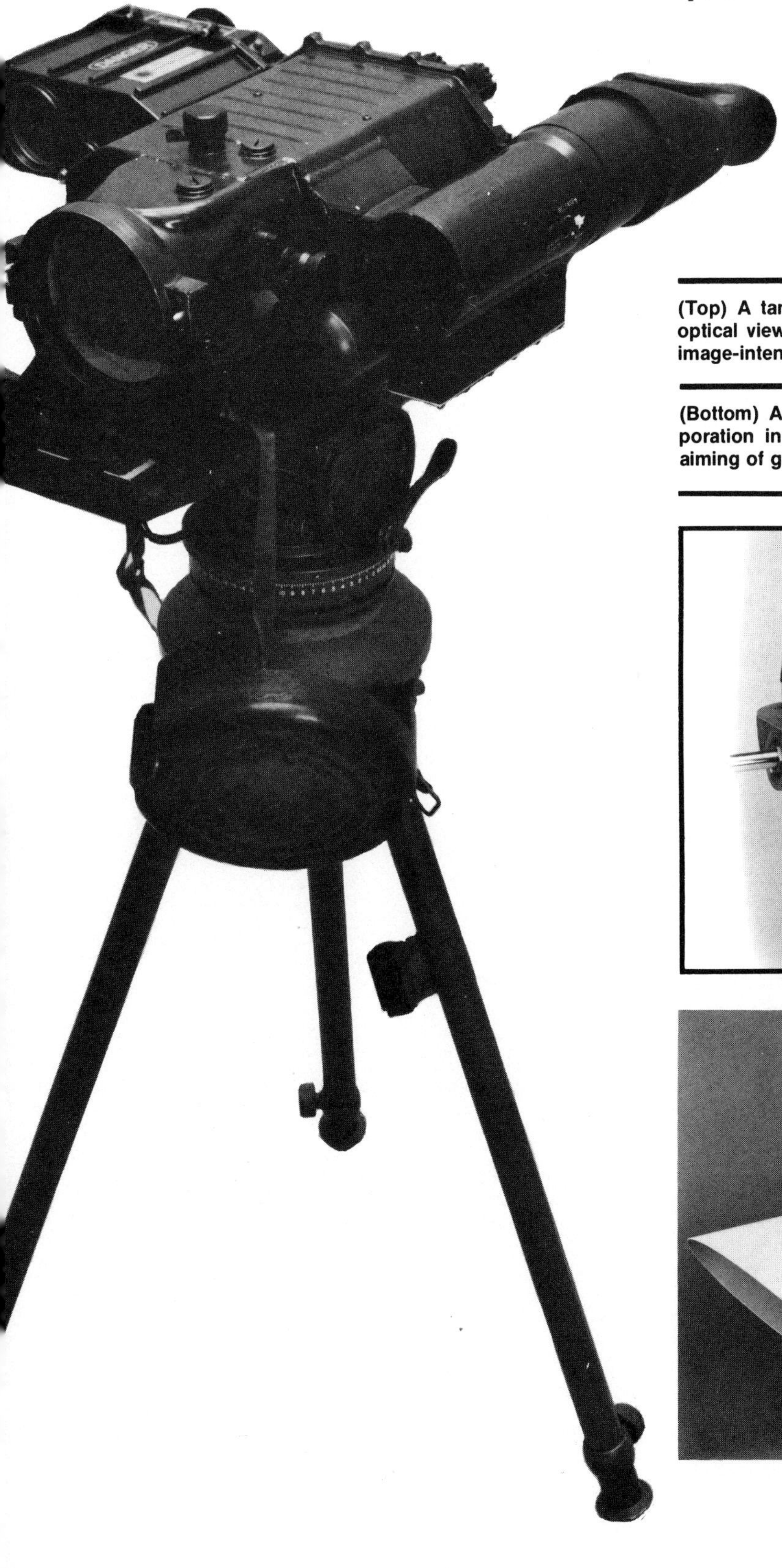

(Top) A tank sighting periscope which incorporates normal optical viewing arrangements for daylight operation with an image-intensifying system allowing night firing

(Bottom) A Philips-Usfa thermal imaging camera for incorporation in various types of fire control systems to permit aiming of guns or missiles at night

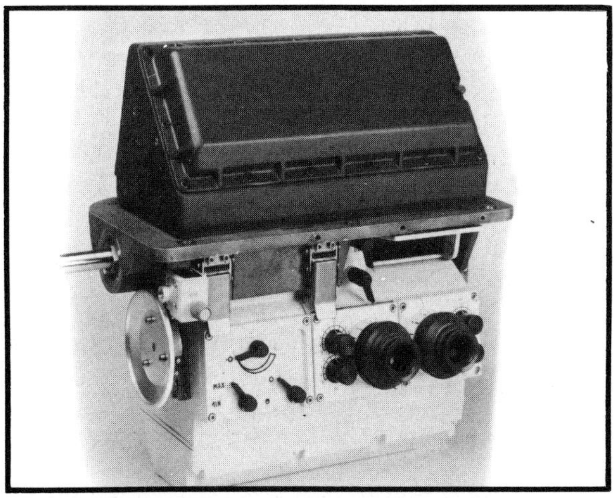

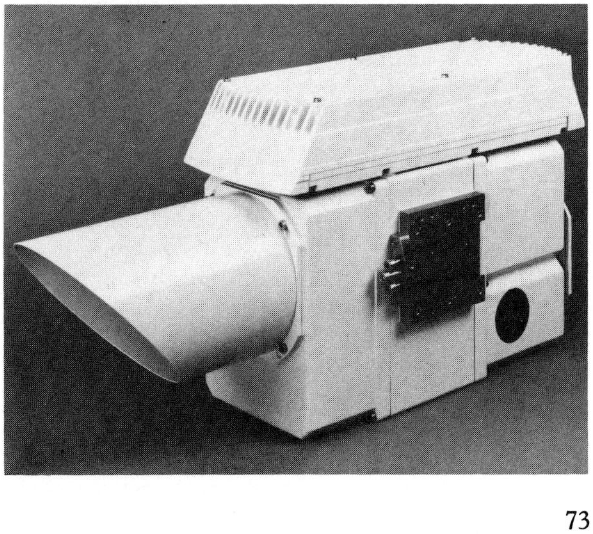

Explosives and Ammunition

The State Of The Art

Ian V. Hogg

Weapons of all kinds have been going through a period of considerable change for the past decade, and this has been fairly faithfully catalogued in print, but weapons are pointless unless they have ammunition, and it seems reasonable to assume that if weapons have been going through a period of change, then so has the ammunition. But we have heard much less of that. Perhaps now is the time to redress the balance.

The textbook case of matching weapon to ammunition and employing new technology on both is that of the Heckler & Koch G-11 rifle. Caseless ammunition is not entirely new; drawings of experimental German rounds surfaced after the last war, though there is little record of the weapons that were meant to go with them. The cartridge consisted of a bullet embedded in a block of propellant explosive, with a percussion cap embedded in the rear of the block. Subsequent developments followed much the same path; in 1959 American technicians at Frankford Arsenal began working on a small-calibre caseless cartridge and some ten years later they had developed a 7.62mm round which, in essence, was a bullet embedded in a block of propellant, with a percussion cap at the rear end.

But inventing the caseless cartridge, or even re-inventing it, is a useless exercise unless a weapon is developed at the same time, and here lay the difficulties. The conventional cartridge case performs a number of useful functions, a major one of which is that of acting as a 'heat sink' to absorb the heat generated by the explosion of the propellant before it can be passed to the metal of the gun barrel. Thus the weapon can fire a large number of rounds before the gun barrel reaches a dangerous temperature. The danger lies in the fact that an extremely hot gun chamber can transmit heat through the cartridge case to the propellant in a freshly loaded cartridge and, if the weapon is not immediately fired, the rise in temperature will ignite the propellant and fire the cartridge – to the surprise and embarrassment of the man holding the weapon.

This phenomenon, called 'cook-off', is well known and in conventional-cartridge weapons has been mastered by careful design of the barrel dimensions. In light machine guns it is done by arranging for the barrel to be changed quickly for a cool one when the danger point is approached. It was this phenomenon which now plagued the caseless cartridge developers, as there was no brass case to act as a heat sink and thus the transfer of heat to the barrel took place at high speed,

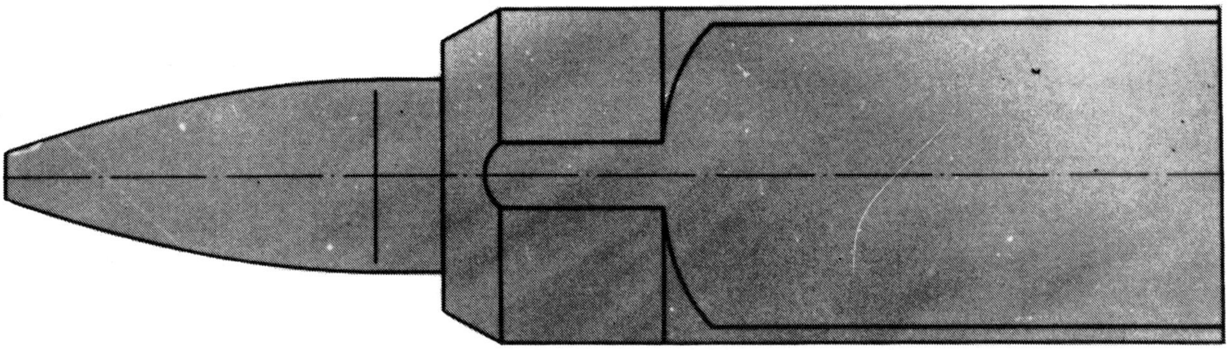

Heckler and Koch's 4.7 mm caseless cartridge

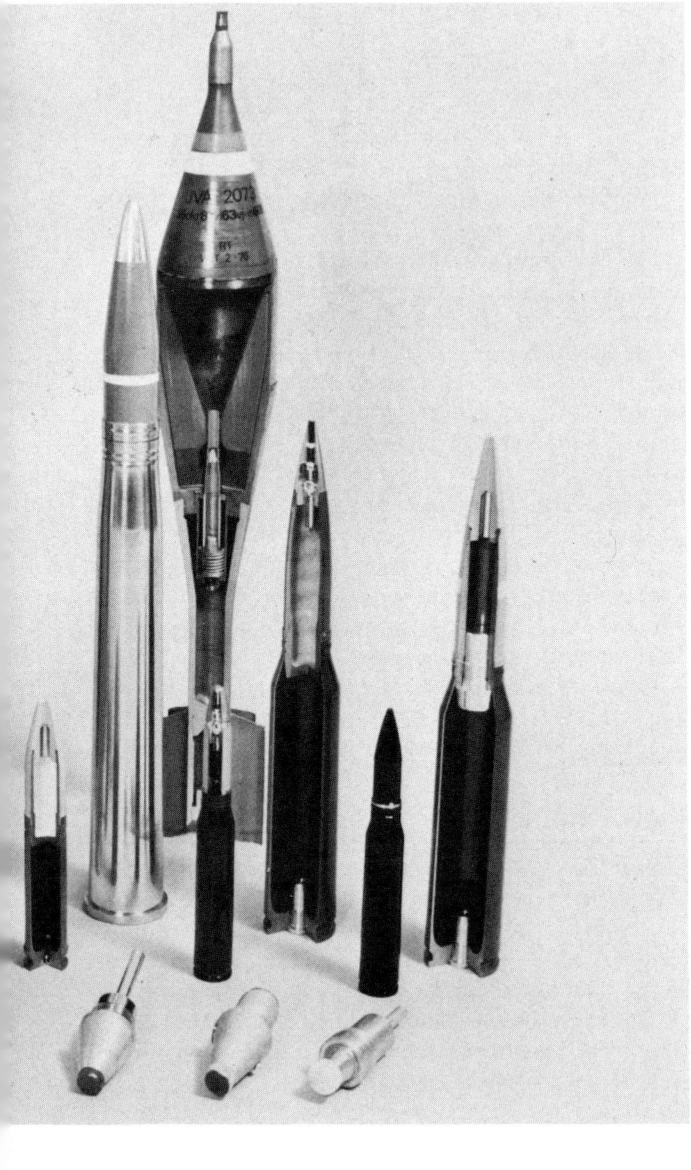

(Left) Valmet Oy's Jyvaskyla Works has been producing ammunition and fuzes ever since 1940

heating up the weapon very rapidly; and as a natural consequence, the reverse transfer, of heat from barrel to naked propellant, also took place rapidly. The result was that caseless weapons cooked-off after a very few shots had been fired. In the absence of any official statement it seems probable that this was one of the major difficulties which led to the abandonment of the caseless programme at Frankford Arsenal.

Others were trying at much the same time. Smith & Wesson had developed a submachine gun with an eye on a possible US Navy contract, a design derived from the Swedish 'Carl Gustaf', and as a sideline they experimented with a version using caseless cartridges fired by electric primers. Work began in 1968 and went on for a few years before being abandoned; again, no reasons were given. At much the same time the Daisy company, well known for air rifles, produced a design in which the cartridge was ignited by a jet of hot air produced by the action of a piston. This was apparently offered commercially for a short time but it too fell by the wayside eventually.

So the question must be how have Heckler & Koch apparently succeeded where others have failed? There are a number of possible reasons, not the least of which is that some 15 years have gone by since the American project was begun and a lot of technology has been soaked up in that time. But certainly one important and pertinent factor is that Heckler & Koch, in collaboration with Dynamit Nobel, have made some fundamental changes in the nature of the propellant.

Earlier caseless cartridges used a block of propellant which was essentially conventional tubular nitrocellulose powder mixed with some form of resinous binder and moulded into shape. Indeed, the first

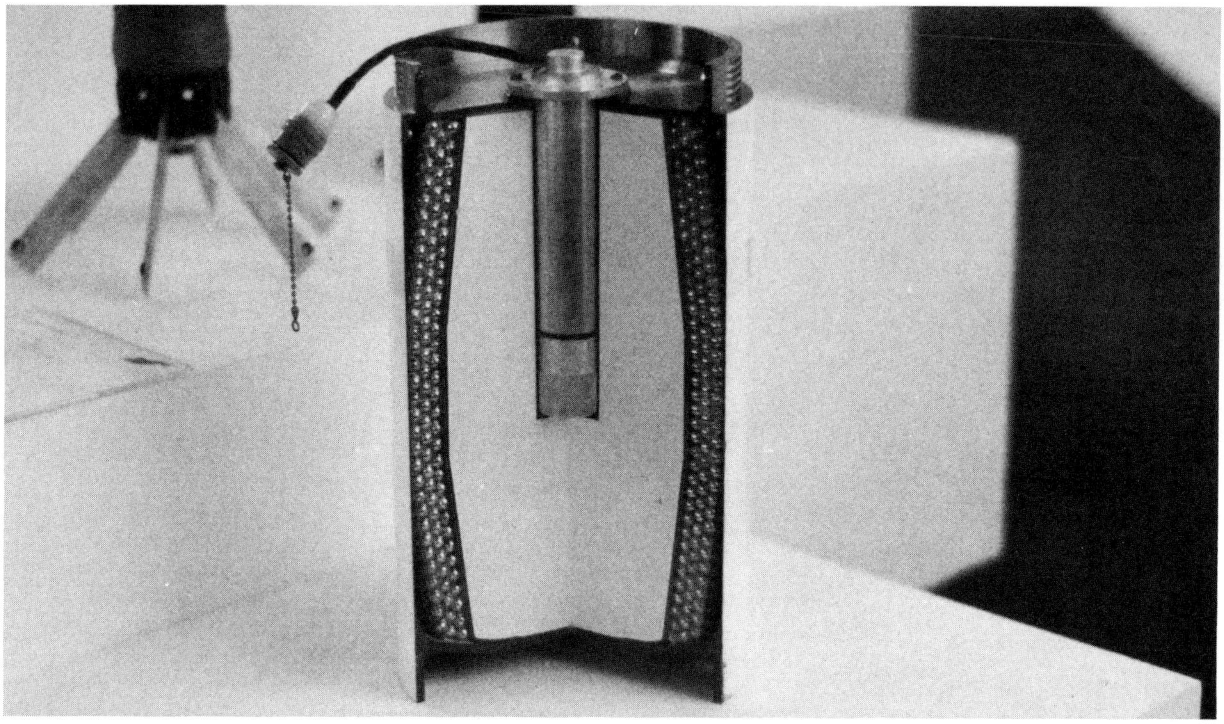

Heckler & Koch/Dynamit Nobel designs did just that. But practical tests showed that the old bogey of cook-off appeared, and so they took a fresh look at the propellant question.

It should be appreciated at the outset that the explosive substance used in propellants needs to have very different characteristics to that used in, say, the bursting charge of a shell or bomb. The propellant needs to **burn** at a regular and controllable, albeit very fast, rate so as to generate gas which can be used to drive the projectile up the gun barrel. The explosive in a shell, on the other hand, **detonates** – undergoes instant molecular disruption – which shatters its casing and develops a powerful blast and shock wave. To detonate an explosive inside a gun chamber is asking for trouble; the rate of detonation is so abrupt that the gun will shatter – which is exactly what happens on the rare occasion that a faulty explosive shell goes off prematurely in a gun barrel.

Due to this basic difference there has always been a distinction between propellant explosives and 'high' explosives, but over the past 30 to 40 years there has been a gradual move towards the incorporation of very small quantities of high explosive into propellant mixes; they are, in spite of their detonating features, attractive since they contain immense amounts of energy in a small space, and if some of this can be tapped for propulsive purposes, so much the better. Indeed, one of the earliest of propellants, Cordite, contained a high proportion of nitro-glycerin for this very reason, but experience showed that powders containing NG had a very high burning temperature and rapidly eroded the gun barrel. Modern research, particularly into improved rocket propellants, led to the use of very finely divided high explosives such as PETN and RDX in propellants, and these produced more acceptable results.

This was the path followed in the case of the G-11 cartridge. A totally new propellant, known as HITP (High Ignition Temperature Propellant) was developed, which was based on a moderated form of the high explosive 'Octagon', itself a relative of the RDX family. The principal advantage has been to raise the ignition temperature so that the cook-off point is some 100°C above that of conventional nitro-cellulose powders. This, of course, raises difficulties with the ignition of the powder by its primer, which appear to have been overcome, probably by the use of some intermediary between the cap and the actual propellant. There are still many things we do not know about the G-11 and its cartridge, details which are carefully guarded by the designers, but there is no doubt that a safe and practical weapon has been achieved, and in no small measure this is due to the successful perfection of the cartridge.

High Explosives

High explosives have been the subject of constant, if low-profile, research over the years, principally with the object of trying to compress as much energy into as small a space as possible. For a long time after the war there was a hiatus in this business, since the power of nuclear explosives had somewhat overawed people, and there were many uncertain statements about 'taming' nuclear materials to make them amenable to being used for minor tasks such as mining and civil engineering.

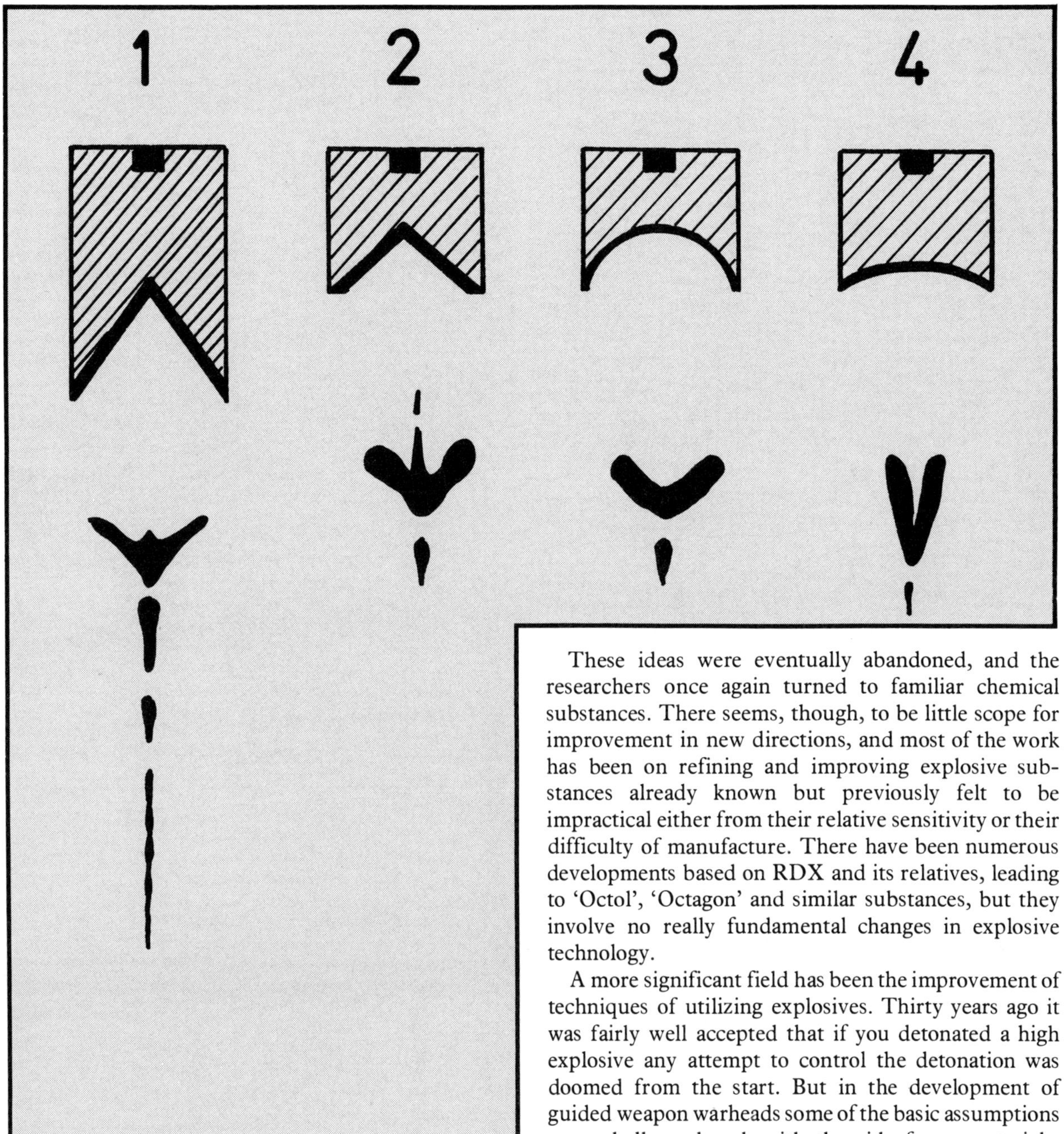

(Top left) An example of modern ammunition technology is this warhead for an Italian 'Aspide' missile. It uses pre-formed fragments set into a plastic wave-shaping matrix so as to control the fragment distribution after detonation takes place

(Above) the differing effects of special charges. 1. Hollow charge; 2. 'P' charge; 3. Schardin charge; 4. Self-forming fragment charge. All charges detonated centrally, from the rear: notice the change in liner deformation

These ideas were eventually abandoned, and the researchers once again turned to familiar chemical substances. There seems, though, to be little scope for improvement in new directions, and most of the work has been on refining and improving explosive substances already known but previously felt to be impractical either from their relative sensitivity or their difficulty of manufacture. There have been numerous developments based on RDX and its relatives, leading to 'Octol', 'Octagon' and similar substances, but they involve no really fundamental changes in explosive technology.

A more significant field has been the improvement of techniques of utilizing explosives. Thirty years ago it was fairly well accepted that if you detonated a high explosive any attempt to control the detonation was doomed from the start. But in the development of guided weapon warheads some of the basic assumptions were challenged and, with the aid of new materials, some very interesting results emerged. For example, in developing the various types of 'rod' warhead, in which a cylinder of explosive was surrounded by longitudinal steel rods, either discrete or with their tips welded together, the central detonation of the explosive led to a spherical blast wave which distorted the rods and reduced their effectiveness as missiles. But by inserting a suitably shaped plastic liner between rods and explosive, it was possible to attenuate the blast wave in certain directions, to 'shape the wave' so that it arrived at the rods in a plane form and thus accelerated the rods outward in an undeformed condition. The next evidence of this was found when Soviet RPG hollow-charge rockets were examined and found to contain plastic wave-shapers which improved the propagation of the wave through the charge and ensured the most effective deformation of the charge liner.

During 1944-45 a German experimenter, Professor Schardin, developed some extremely interesting anti-tank mines, though they were not perfected in time to be used in combat. The basic principle was to use a charge of explosive with a slightly dished face, lined with a dense material, and direct the face at the target. When the explosive was detonated, the liner was projected forward at high speed and would do immense damage to a target at some distance. Some very interesting reports were found after the war which showed a German 'Panther' tank with its front face, some 80mm thick, holed by a Schardin mine at 130ft (40 m) range. Nothing very much was done with the idea for several years, until in the late 1950s British experimenters developed an anti-personnel mine based on Schardin's theories. Nobody seemed interested, but the US took up the idea, finally producing the well known 'Claymore' mine which saw extensive use in Vietnam.

There has now been a revival of the Schardin effect, with variations, principally due to the interest in long-range 'remotely delivered' anti-tank weapons. This led to a demand for some sort of munition which could be detonated in mid-air above the target and propel some effect downwards to damage armour. As a result we now have three slightly different types of device, the 'P Charge', the 'Schardin Charge' and the 'Self-forming Fragment'.

The P (for Plate) Charge is, in effect, a hollow charge in which the angle of the coned liner has been increased to make a wide and shallow cone. On detonation the liner remains more cohesive than that of a hollow charge, and instead of forming into a long jet followed by a slug, forms into a fairly solid mass travelling at about 2000 ft/sec (610 m/sec). The Schardin charge uses a hemispherical liner, while the Self-forming Fragment charge uses a liner which is just slightly dished. These two latter types develop their liners into pointed missiles, moving between 2500 - 4500 ft/sec (762 - 12 200 m/sec) and acting as primitive kinetic-energy projectiles. Over the short ranges involved there is little velocity loss, and on impact with the target they act as any kinetic shot would do, penetrating the plate. Their penetration is rather less than might be achieved by a purpose-designed shot at the same velocity, due to their somewhat arbitrary shaping, but once through the armour their disruptive effect is enormous.

Plate charges have also been adopted for anti-tank mines, since they offer the best chance of success in attacking the undersurface of the tank, the so-called 'belly attack'. Belly attack has always been statistically attractive, since it obviously offers a larger target than does the limited area of the track, and it also offers a better return for energy expended in that it can wreck

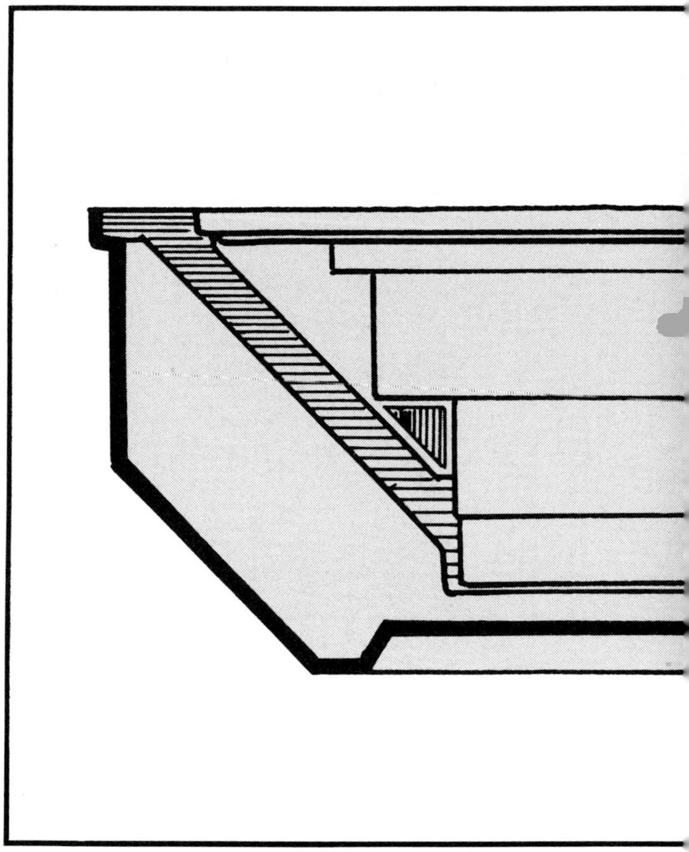

the inside of the tank and kill the crew, whereas breaking a track merely converts a mobile gun-carriage into a static pill-box whose gun can still dominate the immediate area of the battlefield. The technical drawbacks to belly attack were firstly the fuzing of the mine, and secondly the actual mechanics of doing worthwhile amounts of damage with a mine of practical proportions. Burying 100 lb of TNT would have done the trick, but was scarcely a practical proposition.

The plate charge solved this problem since, unlike hollow charge, the plate charge does not demand a finite 'stand-off' distance in which the jet has to be allowed to form before it can penetrate. The plate comes away from its explosive charge formed and ready to penetrate, so that the relatively short travel to the belly of the tank – perhaps 12 – 18 in (30 – 46 cm) – makes no difference to the effect. Fuzing can be achieved by a number of options; pressure hoses which are squeezed by the tank tracks when the mine is straddled, vertical rods tipped by the tank hull, audio, magnetic or vibration sensors – there are several methods available. One slight drawback found in early trials was that if the mine was properly buried, the overlay of soil could interfere with the action of the plate, and so it has become usual to put an 'uncovering charge' on the upper side of the mine; this is fired a few micro-seconds before the main charge, so that it removes the top cover and leaves the way clear for the plate to accelerate when the main charge fires.

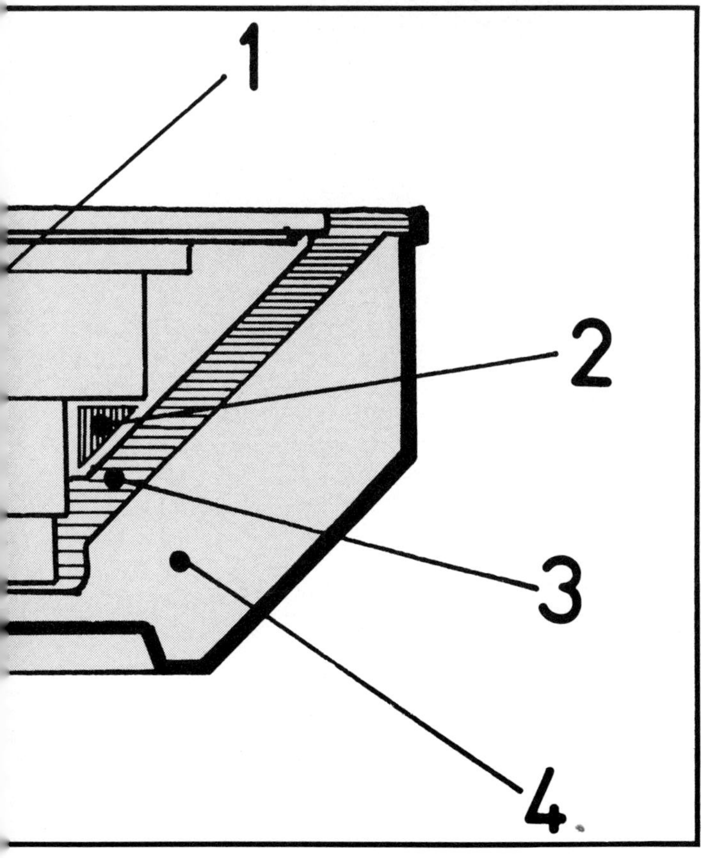

Artillery Shells

Artillery projectiles have been receiving a great deal of attention during the past decade, the object being to increase the range and thus the area commanded by the gun. Today's battlefield inhibits the clustering of artillery, so that giving the individual gun a greater command means increasing the effectiveness of artillery by a sizeable factor. The loss-leader in this promotion is, of course, the rocket-boosted shell; it is a loss-leader because there are formidable problems associated with making it work well and although its supporters are always ready to quote impressive (and genuine) gains in range, they are generally less ready to quote precise figures for accuracy at the extended-range target.

All artillery shells yaw to a greater or lesser amount during the first part of their flight, and the accuracy of a rocket-assisted projectile depends largely upon how well the designer can damp out that yaw before the rocket is ignited. If the axis of the projectile is yawing off the theoretical line of the trajectory at the moment of ignition, then the thrust will tend to perpetuate the

(Top) A French Giat off-route anti-tank mine using plate charge principles, together with an example of its effect on armour plate.

(Left) The Swedish FFV-028 belly-attack mine uses the Schardin plate effect. 1. Fuse; 2. Uncovering charge; 3. Plate; 4. Bursting charge

error. It is to the credit of all concerned that the current offerings in this field are as good as they are. A more serious objection, some feel, is that too much of the shell's mass is occupied by the rocket propellant and its ancillary timing and igniting devices. The rocket assistance unit for the American 155mm M549A1 shell, for example, takes up 29.8 lbs (13.5 kg) and 10.5 in (26.7 cm) of the shell, and in order to get a worthwhile bursting charge into what remains it is necessary to use a higher grade steel for the shell body than is necessary with a conventional shell.

An alternative method of obtaining more range is the use of the 'base bleed' technique, and this is rapidly gaining adherents. Briefly, this involves burning a pyrotechnic substance in a chamber at the rear of the shell so as to emit gases which fill the vacuum generated at the base during flight. Properly done, this can reduce drag by about 50 per cent and add some 10 – 15 per cent to the range. Another method is to burn the same type

(Below) General Defence Corporation's 155 mm Rocket Assisted Projectile's motor body

(Left) Belgian 'EFRB' (extended range, full bore) 155 mm projectile, using a hemispherical base to reduce drag and aerodynamic stub wings to give added lift during flight plus stability in the gun barrel

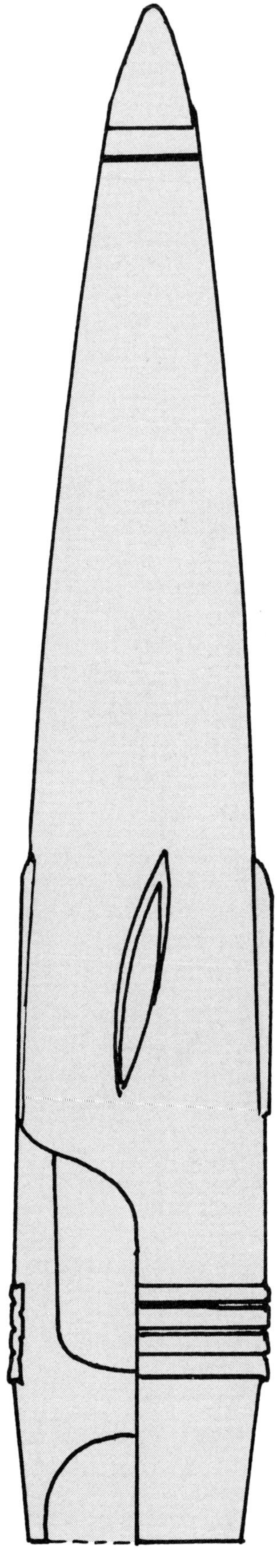

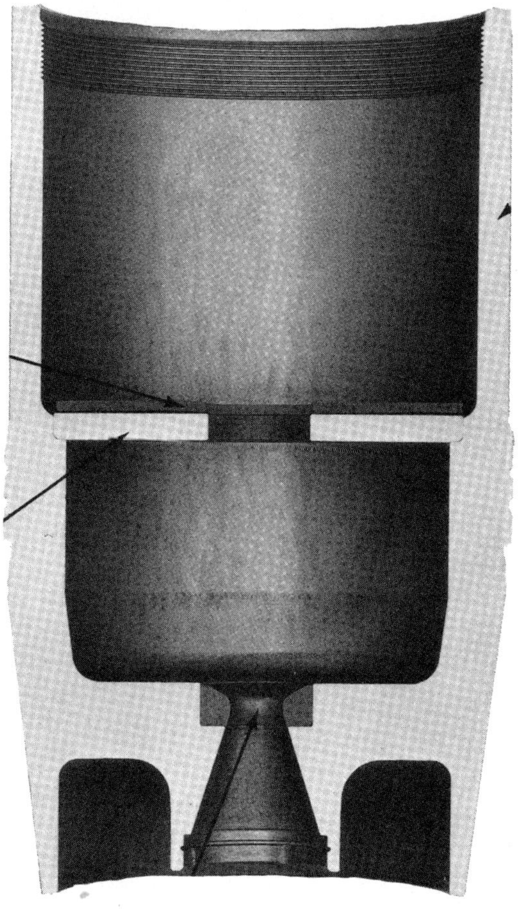

of substance but allow the gases to leak out through a number of peripheral holes so as to flow back over the rear surface of the shell and then into the vacuum area. This technique capitalizes on the 'boundary layer' effect to reduce skin drag as well as base drag; at present this system is in the early stages of exploration and nobody is prepared to give estimates on the sort of range increase which might be expected. It is not without interest to recall that this idea was put forward as far back as 1918, called the 'Chilowski effect', but at that time so little was known of aerodynamics that it had no success. It was revived in 1940, still without attracting official interest. We can only hope that 'third time lucky' holds good in this case.

Ballistic shaping also has its effects on extending range, particularly by designing a long and tapering nose and base. This, unfortunately, leaves very little parallel-sided portion of the shell to give it a bearing surface during its passage up the bore, and it therefore becomes necessary to support the nose during this period. An interesting design has appeared in Belgium in which the nose support comes from four aerodynamic stub wings on the ogive; these are canted, to match the airflow over the spinning shell, and after supporting and steadying the shell in the barrel they give aerodynamic lift during flight.

These shells also incorporate another structural device coming into very common use, the 'hemispherical base' in which the rear end of the shell is formed into a hollow hemisphere instead of being simply and abruptly terminated at right-angles to the longitudinal axis. This again is a device for reducing base drag, and appears to work very well, giving an increase of some 10 per cent in range without the need for any mechanical or pyrotechnic complications. The Belgian shell, using both the hemispherical base and the aerodynamic stub wings, in conjunction with a very smooth shape, gives increases of 15 - 20 per cent of range, depending upon which model of 155 mm howitzer is used.

Conclusion

In the space at our disposal we have been able only to scratch the surface of current explosive and ammunition development; furthermore, of course, there must be a good deal of work going on behind closed doors of which we cannot be aware and which will only become apparent in the future. We have not discussed, for example, current trends in discarding sabot ammunition, both in the anti-tank field and, perhaps less well known, in the anti-personnel field; internal security demands have led to many developments in chemical and other munitions for riot control; and mention of chemical riot control leads us to think about the whole clouded subject of chemical munitions for military operations. All these, and several other related subjects, we hope to discuss in the future.

Tank Guns for Future Main Battle Tanks

Geoffrey Tillotson

The current debate over the form of future Main Battle Tanks (MBTs) centres, as ever, on the traditional attributes of armour, namely firepower, mobility and protection. Nearly 70 years have passed since the tank made its hesitant debut at Flers and during this time the design of MBTs has more or less crystallized into the form which is recognized today, that is, a tracked chassis, a revolving manned turret with high velocity gun and the use of massive armour protection. Any exceptions to this general rule have been made with a particular role in mind, such as the Swedish S Tank or the German JPz Kan Tank Destroyer.

In recent years there have been many advances in engines, transmissions and suspensions which have had their effect upon the design of tanks. For example, it has been possible to design powerplants specifically for

tanks and these highly stressed engines do indeed develop very high powers and torques from relatively small volumes. Greatly reduced fuel consumption and highly efficient cooling systems mean that less space and therefore less weight has to be allocated to these factors, while transmissions have also benefited from advances in automotive technology. Sophisticated suspensions allow cross-country speeds to be raised until the tolerance of the crew to shaking about becomes the limiting factor, but at the same time the increase in agility adds to the passive protection of the tank.

In a similar vein, the past decade has seen major innovations in the design and application of armour materials to tanks. The exact details of modern compound armours are rightly not disclosed in open literature, but it appears that the major tank-producing countries of the West have each developed and introduced a compound armour of one form or another, while the Soviet Union is widely reported to employ its own type of composite armour in the design of the T-72 and T-64 main battle tanks.

In the absence of precise details of the construction or performance of these advanced armours it is only possible to speculate on their effect on tank design. However, testimony before the Congressional Armed Services Committee in 1979 indicated that neither the TOW nor the HOT missile warheads could penetrate the frontal armour of the Soviet T-72 tank, and it is clear that in the West there has been a major thrust to boost the performance of the entire spectrum of anti-tank weapons. Since the principal tank-killing weapon

This prototype of the Challenger MBT is armed with the L11A5 120 mm rifled gun, although it is intended that later production Challengers will have the UK's new high pressure rifled gun, which will also be retrofitted to existing Chieftains and Challengers of earlier production. In this photograph the bore evacuator (fume extractor) can be seen approximately halfway down the barrel, with the 2 halves of the thermal insulation jacket on either side. The object at the muzzle is the protective guard for the Muzzle Reference Sight (Crown Copyright)

on the battlefield is the tank itself, it is hardly surprising that a good deal of this effort should be concentrated on tank guns.

This article sets out to describe the weapons which have been selected as the main armament of the 'follow-on' generation of MBTs, that is, the tanks which are about to enter service or are under development. From these descriptions it is intended to identify the areas of broad agreement and also those areas where there is disagreement, whether minor or fundamental. The latter points will then be reviewed in the light of the threat which tank guns must counter.

As a starting point it is assumed that there is no need to recount the recent history of tank guns, except to establish a baseline for these discussions, and that the functioning of the major kinetic energy (KE) and chemical energy (CE) forms of armour-defeating ammunition is understood. It is also necessary to make another disclaimer. Regrettably, the scope of this article does not permit coverage of the other advances which are also being made in the field of firepower. Nevertheless, it is worth listing some of these as an indication of the wide range of factors which affect the selection of a tank gun. They include:

- The application of liquid propellants to tank guns.
- The development of advanced materials such as Electroslag Refined Steels for tank guns.
- The development of advanced materials such as high alloy steels, tungsten-nickel alloys, tungsten carbide and depleted uranium alloys for KE penetrators.
- The size of the gun and the space available within the turret. As calibre increases, so the size of the complete round increases and it may be necessary to separate the projectile and the propelling charge. The design of the breech then becomes of importance.
- The wider use of high energy propellants, which are in effect high explosives.
- The possibility of terminal guidance or homing for tank gun-launched projectiles.
- The interaction of the tank fire control system with the gun, which may include the ability to send fuzing information to a projectile in flight.
- The combination of KE and CE techniques, as in

the Rheinmetall proposal for a discarding sabot-type of penetrator mounted ahead of a hollow charge.

Conventional field artillery guns have nearly always been rifled, and since the first tank guns were merely adaptations of artillery weapons and gave satisfactory results, there was no particular motivation to question the requirement for rifled guns or to consider smoothbore guns. By the end of the Second World War it was possible to achieve a very satisfactory performance with armour-piercing ammunition fired from tank guns and the use of the shaped charge effect in High Explosive Antitank (HEAT) projectiles meant that the armour designer had two separate threats to consider.

By the mid-1950s the Armour Piercing Discarding Sabot (APDS) projectile, fired from a rifled gun, was the most potent armour-defeating ammunition at the disposal of a tank commander. The APDS projectile comprises a core, or 'penetrator', of dense, hard material, which is propelled from the gun at a high velocity by means of a light carrier, or 'sabot' which is discarded at the muzzle. The core relies on spin imparted in the gun before sabot discard for its stability as it flies to the target, so while a high ratio of length to diameter (L/D) is desirable for good penetration in terms of the force which can be exerted over a given contact area, there is a practical limit of about six to one above which the projectile becomes unstable in flight.

(Below) The L11 series 120 mm rifled gun, which is produced at ROF Nottingham, in the final stages of manufacture (ROF Nottingham)

(Left) The Chieftain 900 MBT has been developed as a private venture by ROF Leeds and is also armed with the L11A5 gun (ROF Leeds)

To exceed this limit requires another type of stability, and fins are the most obvious form. However, if a fin-stabilized projectile is fired from a rifled gun there will be an unacceptable loss of energy in imparting unnecessary spin to this heavier projectile. One way out of this dilemma was to use a non-rifled or smoothbore gun.

Interest in smoothbore guns in the West dates back to 1949 when the US Ordnance Technical Committee approved an extended development programme for several tank guns of different types and calibres. As part of this programme, development of the T208 90 mm smoothbore gun began in 1954. This gun, intended for the T95 medium tank, was designed with the aim of penetrating 5 inches (127 mm) of armour inclined at 60 degrees at a range of 2000 yards (1830 m). Although over 80 different models of the T320 'Arrow Shot' Armour-Piercing Fin-Stabilized Discarding Sabot (APFSDS) projectile were tested, the lack of understanding of penetration mechanisms and material properties prevented the Ordnance Corps from achieving any degree of consistency. The T208 gun effectively

(Right) The first 3000 production M1 Abrams MBTs for the US Army will be fitted with the M68E1 105mm rifled gun, which is closely related to the British L7 gun. The gun of the M1, firing the current M774 round, is considered by the US Army to be the equal of any present APFSDS penetrator, and the planned XM833 replacement should maintain this posture until the M1A1 tank, with the German 120 mm smoothbore gun, is available in sufficient numbers to meet the threat. The tank illustrated is an early XM1 pre-production model (US Army)

(Below) The L7A3 105 mm rifled gun is widely used throughout NATO and the Free World. The eccentrically-located bore evacuator is a characteristic of this gun (ROF Nottingham)

stood or fell by the success of the Arrow Shot, the first 'Long Rod Penetrator', so when this failed to meet the requirement the US turned to the British L28 105 mm APDS round for its next MBT, the M60. The M68 gun, type classified in August 1959, was therefore designed to be interchangeable with the British L7 barrel.

With such intensive research in progress in the United States into long rod penetrators it would have been remarkable if the Soviet Union had overlooked this approach. As it turned out, their research had been considerably more successful, and the T-62 MBT, introduced in 1965, was equipped with a 115 mm smoothbore gun.

By the mid-1960s there were thus 3 significant tank guns in service throughout the world. The British L7 105 mm rifled gun (or the American M68) was accepted as the standard NATO tank gun. It was provided with highly effective APDS and HESH (HEP, in US terminology) rounds. Although not required by British doctrine, an American-designed fin-stabilized HEAT round was also available. This round, the M456, used the principle of the slipping driving band to reduce the amount of spin imparted by the rifling of the gun. In this way the degradation in performance due to rotation of the shaped charge could be kept to a minimum.

The Soviet U-5T 115 mm smoothbore gun in the T-62, while not yet in widespread use, could fire APFSDS, HEAT-FS and HE-FS, the latter two being fitted with folding fins. In the 1973 Yom Kippur War the BR-6 APFSDS shot of the U-5T gun was found to be extremely effective; indeed, until recently, US Army pamphlets described it as '. . . the fastest tank cannon in the world' and '. . . extremely accurate out to . . . 1500 meters'.

Paradoxically, although the British L7 gun was widely acclaimed throughout NATO, it was no longer current in the UK, for the Chieftain MBT with its L11 gun had replaced the 105 mm gun Centurion. An extensive range of ammunition was provided for the L11 120 mm rifled gun, but in accordance with British practice, the secondary for Chieftain was HESH, rather than HEAT. When it was introduced, the performance of the L15 APDS shot was outstanding and even today it presents a serious threat to any modern MBT, but to improve the kill probability of the Chieftain against compound armours an APFSDS shot has recently been introduced.

A salutary mention should be made here of the French CN-105-F1 gun which equips the AMX-30. French designers chose to optimize their 105 mm gun for the HEAT round, and this was achieved by adopting a shallower twist in the rifling. As a result, the amount of spin imparted to the projectile is much less and this, combined with the novel technique of mounting the shaped charge in ball races, means that the HEAT round suffers very little of the degradation normally associated with projectiles of this type. However, against the perceived advantages of logistical, tactical and training simplicity in having only one type of

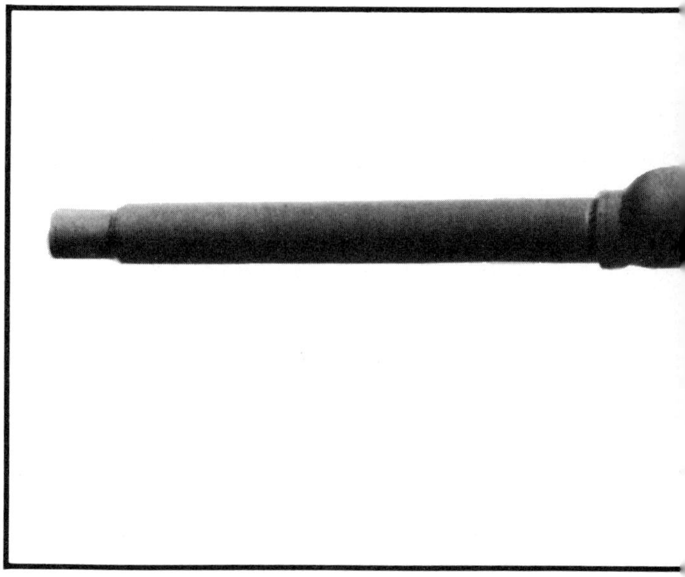

DM13 APFSDS (left) and HEAT-MP (right) rounds for the German 120 mm gun are manufactured by Diehl. Only the metal stub case at the base of the round remains in the gun after firing, thus greatly reducing the problem of disposing of empty cases within the tank (Rheinmetall GmbH)

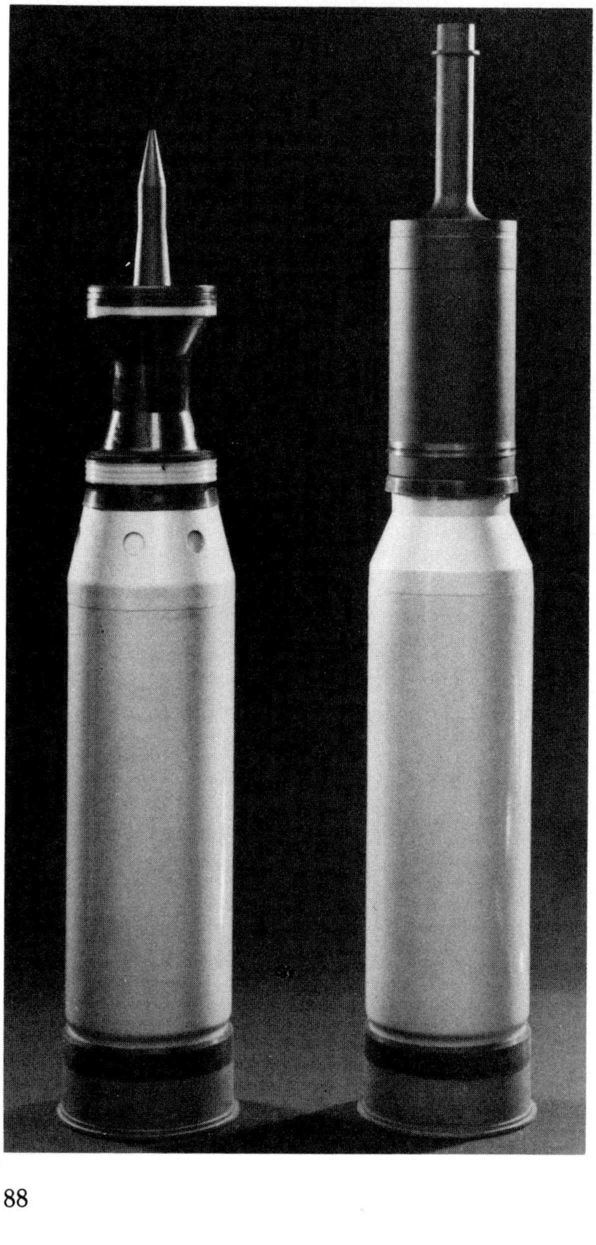

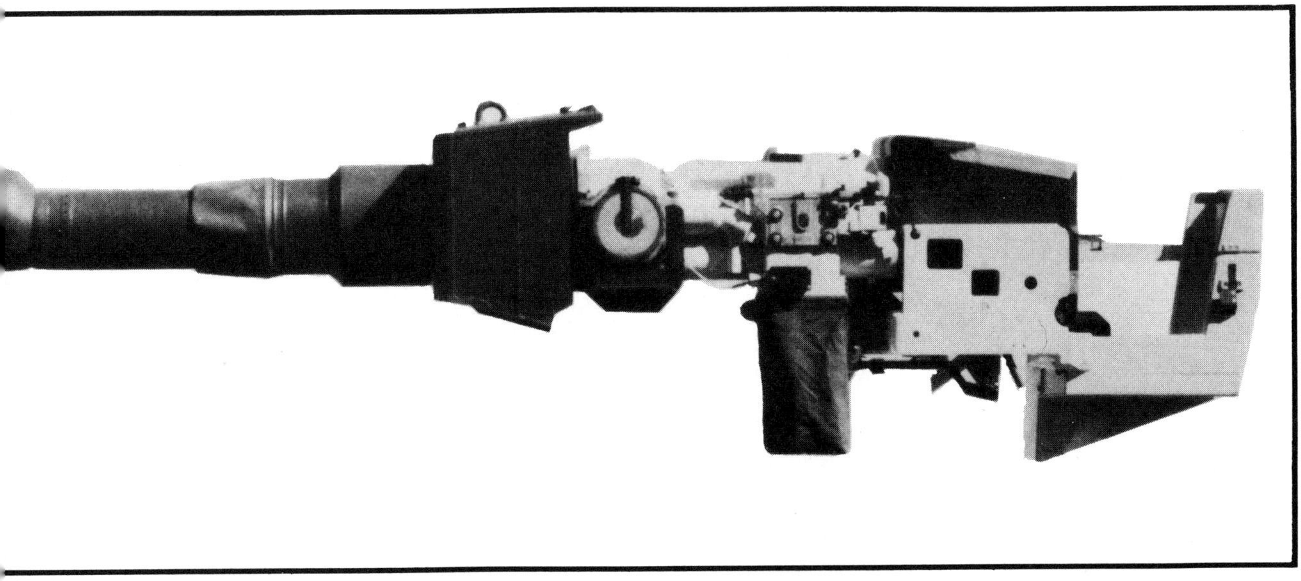

(Above) Rheinmetall's 120 mm smoothbore gun, which is fitted to the Leopard 2. When installed in the US M1E1 prototype it has the designation XM256. The barrel and offset bore evacuator are enclosed in a fibreglass-sheathed insulating sleeve (Rheinmetall GmbH)

(Left) In this sectioned view of the Leopard 2 MBT the 120 mm smoothbore gun and its ammunition stowage can be seen, although the rounds shown appear to be a stylized hybrid between the APFSDS and the HEAT-MP cartridges. It would be preferable to follow the British practice and stow the HEAT-MP rounds in the hull to minimize the risk of turret fires if hit (Krauss-Maffei)

round, the assumption that HEAT would retain its effectiveness is seriously challenged by modern armours, and the lack of suitable rifling for APDS is a grave omission. The recent announcement of an APFSDS round for this gun will therefore have been welcomed.

The Federal Republic of Germany (FRG) adopted the British L7A3 gun for its Leopard 1 series of MBTs. The successor to the Leopard was intended to be the joint US/FRG MBT-70/KPz 70 tank, and for this project Germany had accepted the US 152 mm rifled gun-launcher. However, despite the fact that an effective APFSDS round, the XM578, had been developed for this gun, the FRG still had reservations about the choice of weapon. When the MBT-70 programme was dropped in 1969 and the FRG pressed ahead with its own Leopard 2 project, a new high velocity gun was required. Given a free hand and the requirement to fire only KE and HEAT ammunition, it is hardly surprising that the designers at Rheinmetall selected a smoothbore solution. The Rheinmetall 120 mm gun equips the Leopard 2 MBT and has also been adopted by the United States (as the XM256) for the M1A1 model of the Abrams MBT, due to enter production in 1984.

Capitalizing on the success of the T-62, yet at the same time incorporating many lessons observed from Western tank development, the Soviet Union has

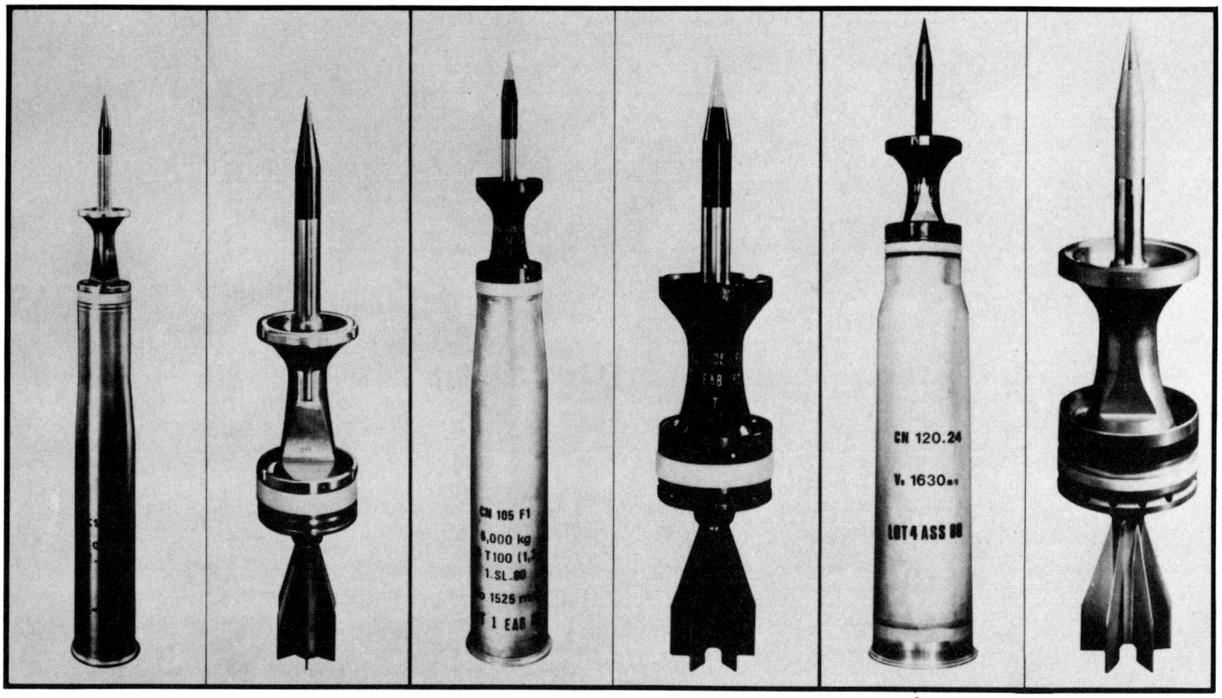

evolved two new tanks, the T-72 and the T-64. While there are doubts over the status of each tank relative to the other, in both cases the gun is a 125 mm smoothbore.

France is known to have a 120 mm smoothbore gun in advanced development, while Japan, Sweden and Switzerland have all indicated their intention to use this type of gun in future MBTs.

In dignified isolation, the United Kingdom still pins its hopes on the rifled gun. The impressive performance and reputation of the L11 gun of the Chieftain suggested to UK designers that a similar or even better performance could be achieved by the use of more energetic propellant in a smaller gun. This would not only reduce weight but would also permit the use of fixed rounds, for although the British Army finds the separate combustible charge cases of the L11 gun no inconvenience, there may have been a degree of resistance to this concept in the minds of other potential customers.

Thus at the 1975 Tripartite Tank Gun Evaluation, the UK entered a new 110 mm rifled gun, together with APFSDS, HESH and HEAT ammunition. Germany's entry was the Rheinmetall 120 mm smoothbore, while the United States entered a new APFSDS round, the XM735, for the existing M68 tank gun. The results of the trial have been the subject of much debate; however, both Germany and the United States adopted their own candidate systems while the UK proceeded with further development of rifled 120 mm guns.

A further shoot-off in 1977 between the UK M13A 120 mm rifled gun (designed to be compatible with the US XM1 MBT then under final development), the German 120 mm smoothbore and the

(Top) GIAT, the French nationalized armament concern, has developed APFSDS rounds in 90 mm (left), 105 mm (centre) and 120 mm (right) calibres. The 90 mm round is intended for the F4 gun which equips the Sagaie wheeled tank destroyer, while the 105 mm round provides a KE capability for the gun of the AMX-30 MBT. The 120 mm round, which is compatible with the German round, is intended for the next French MBT, the EPC, and for the AMX-32 (GIAT)

(Above) The M774 105 mm APFSDS projectile is currently the standard KE round within the US Army. It has a monobloc penetrator of DU and reduced-drag fins (US Army)

The US M735 105 mm APFSDS round is manufactured by General Defense. The penetrator contains a tungsten-nickel-iron core within an aerodynamic sheath. The gas bleed passages which assist in sabot discard can be seen at the rear of each of the 3 sabot petals. The M735A1 round contains a penetrator of depleted uranium (DU) but although type classified shortly after the M735, it was not produced in quantity. General Defense, formerly known as Flinchbaugh, has also developed private venture APFSDS rounds in 76 mm, 90 mm and 105 mm calibres (General Defense)

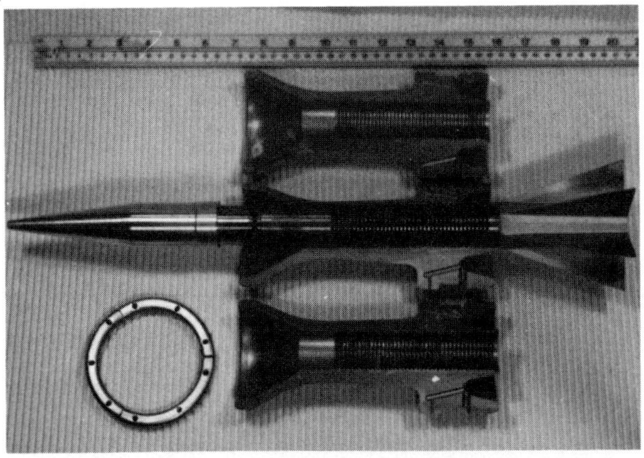

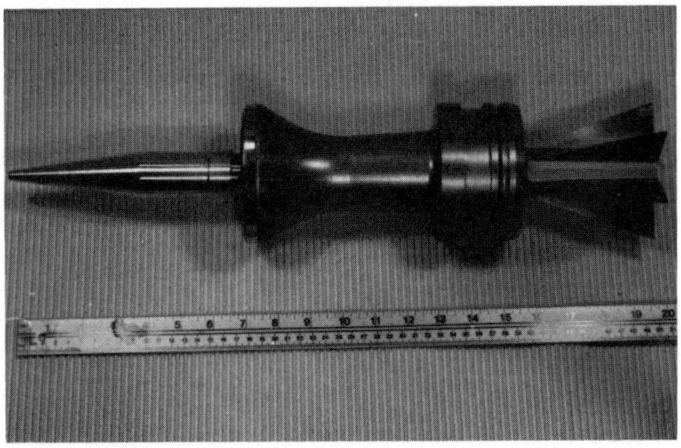

United States XM774 APFSDS round with depleted uranium penetrator, ended in a similar stalemate. The US took the view that any target which could defeat 105 mm KE attack could probably defeat the 120 mm guns as well, so in the short term it was acceptable to continue with the M68 gun and the excellent XM774 round. For the longer term it selected the German 120 mm gun, as described earlier. Despite the apparent effectiveness of the XM774 round and the potential of its successors under development, the M68 gun cannot be considered as a real contender for a follow-on MBT and for this reason it will not be discussed further in this article.

The UK M13A gun, which was rejected by the United States in favour of the German gun, was considerably shorter than the L11 yet fired APFSDS at a higher pressure. By designing a new high pressure gun of approximately the same length as the L11 the UK has produced a gun which is compatible with existing L11 ammunition and mountings, as well as with the

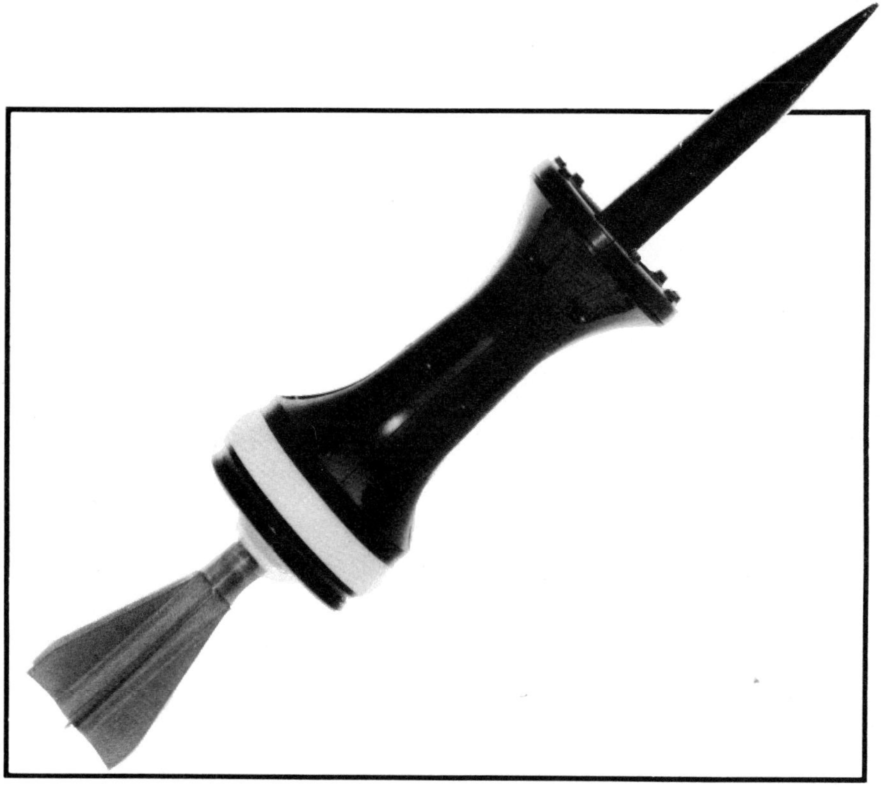

(Left) The US XM833 105 mm APFSDS projectile is planned to succeed the M735 and M774 projectiles. Its monobloc penetrator is made of DU and has a greater L/D ratio than previous penetrators (US Army)

(Centre) The initial KE capability of the M1A1 MBT will be provided by an Americanized version of the German DM13 round, designated XM827 in US service. It differs from the DM13 in that a monobloc DU core is used in the steel-sheathed penetrator in place of the 2-piece tungsten alloy core of the German projectile. The prime contractor for the XM827 round is Honeywell (US Army)

(Right) Eventually, the standard KE round for the M1A1 MBT will be the XM829 shown here. The final form of the sabot is as yet uncertain, and recent information suggests that it will be considerably shorter than that shown in this photograph (US Army)

mounting in the Challenger MBT, while having a greatly improved performance. This gun, with the experimental designation EXP 32M1, fires APFSDS and an improved HESH which has a better ballistic shape and possibly improved fuzing. Interestingly, the M13A gun designed with the XM1 tank in mind had been provided with APFSDS and a fin-stabilized HEAT round.

From the present state of the art, it is now possible to determine two major points of agreement:

- The primary armour-defeating round must be APFSDS.
- The gun must have a calibre of at least 120 mm.

At the same time, there are substantial differences in opinion, and these centre on two aspects:

- The selection of a secondary armour-defeating round.
- Whether the gun should be rifled or smoothbore.

An examination of the threat posed by future MBTs reveals several factors which influence the choice of weapon and ammunition. Many of these bear out the two major points of agreement. For example, the use of sophisticated fire control systems means that targets can, and therefore must, be engaged at greater ranges. At the same time these targets will be more agile and may only expose themselves for brief periods. A short time of flight is thus required to ensure a hit, and this leads to the KE solution, while in general terms the greater range requires a larger gun. The KE solution also permits a higher rate of observed fire in these circumstances.

Other factors are open to different interpretations. These centre on the use of compound armours and the requirement to engage secondary targets.

It is widely accepted that the long rod penetrator gives the best chance of penetrating modern armours. It is also generally thought that the inclusion of ceramics, light metals and plastics in these compound systems will tend to dissipate the jet of hot particles produced by the HEAT projectile, making it ineffective – at least in calibres below 150-160 mm, and the wider use of auxiliary skirting plates adds to the problems facing HEAT. On the other hand, while the effectiveness of HESH against sophisticated armours may be reduced, its effect on any item of equipment outside the armour envelope is devastating. No-one who has seen the results of HESH fired at a tank target will be in any doubt that the vehicle is no longer a viable fighting unit. A hit on the turret will (if it fails to dislodge the turret) destroy all fire control optics, sensors and antennas, possibly also jamming the main armament, while a hit on the hull will almost certainly destroy enough running gear to immobilize the tank.

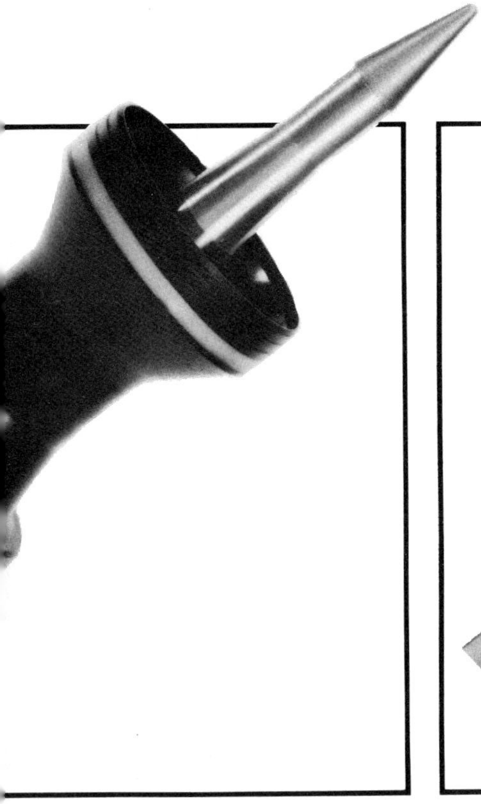

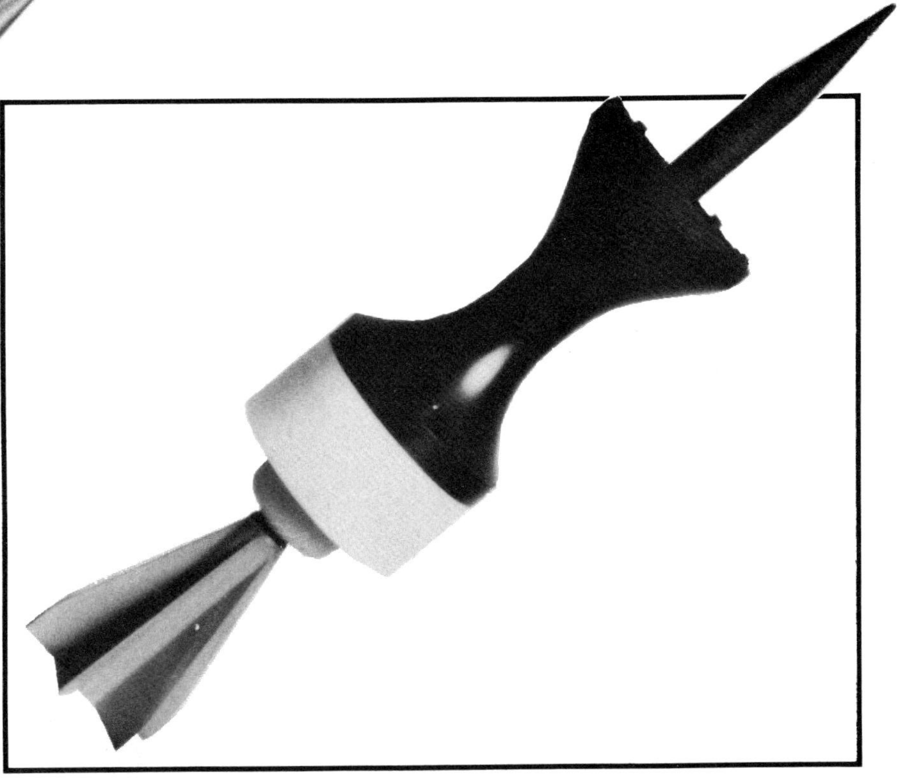

Relative Merits of Fin- and Spin-Stabilization

Factor	Fin-Stabilization	Spin-Stabilization
Secondary Armour Defeating Natures	*HEAT-MP:* probably defeated by compound armour and skirting plates. Adequate against secondary targets. Advanced fuzing techniques may improve performance. *HESH:* impracticable, as the addition of fins would degrade accuracy and reduce explosive payload.	*HEAT:* at present, HESH preferred to HEAT by UK but HEAT could be introduced if necessary. Slipping driving band and fins required. *HESH:* effective against external tank components; excellent against secondary targets.
Other Natures	*Smoke* *HE* *Canister* — require bulky fins, thus less payload and impaired accuracy. HEAT-MP may suffice in lieu of canister.	*Smoke* *Canister* — ballistically similar to HESH. No requirement for HE. Spin aids in dispensing canister payload; may be used in anti-helicopter role.
Arming	Only 2 stimuli (setback, creep) available.	Additional stimulus of spin available as safety interlock.
Sensing	— possible top attack of armour by CE	Controlled spin rate may allow sensing for possible top attack of armour by CE projectile.
Sabot Discard	—	Additional spin assists in clean discard of sabot petals at muzzle.
Muzzle Velocity	No theoretical limit.	Slipping driving band may impose practical upper limit on firing of KE projectiles.
Gun Manufacture	Possibly simpler to build, but precise control of surface finish essential.	Established manufacturing techniques for rifled guns do not present problems.

Considerable interest has been aroused by the 75 mm automatic gun developed by ARES, Inc at Port Clinton, Ohio. It fires 'telescoped' APFSDS rounds in which the projectile is almost completely encased in the propellant in the cartridge case. By this means it is easier to incorporate automatic loading, allowing a high rate of fire. Although the gun has a respectable armour-defeating capability, it is seen more as a useful addition to the fire power of light forces, such as the Rapid Deployment Force, or in urban operations, than as an antiarmour weapon. The gun is 5.67 m long and its low trunnion reaction (recoil force) of some 133.5 kN (30,000 lb) means that it can be mounted in vehicles much lighter than current MBTs (ARES, Inc)

There will always be a need to engage other opportunity targets, such as light armoured vehicles, logistic vehicles and defensive positions. Against such targets the multipurpose HEAT (HEAT-MP) round developed for the German 120 mm smoothbore gun has a useful potential which is further increased by the fragmentation effect of the charge casing against personnel. Once again, the effect of HESH is superior due to its greater explosive content, and it is inherently more accurate at longer ranges. It is also considerably cheaper to manufacture!

The key to the dilemma appears to be the internal ballistics associated with the APFSDS projectile. Originally the rifled gun offered a 3-pronged attack: APDS, HEAT and HESH. In the case of HEAT, it was necessary to use a slipping driving band to decouple the projectile from the rotation imparted in the rifling and a finned empennage to stabilize the projectile in flight. (The penetration is seriously degraded if the rotation of the hollow charge exceeds 20 rpm.) With the advent of the fin-stabilized long rod penetrator it appeared more convenient and less of a technological risk to go to a smoothbore gun, accepting that it would not be possible to fire conventional spin-stabilized projectiles. This did not just mean abandoning HESH, but it also forced the development of fin-stabilized smoke, illuminating, HE and canister rounds if these were still required. It should be noted that the FRG had not specified 'special purpose' ammunition other than KE and HEAT for the 120 mm smoothbore gun, and considered that HESH was no longer significant due to the use of spaced

armour. The German designers also drew on their experience with 90 mm and 105 mm HEAT manufacture and concluded that the interdependence of the high pressures, the rifling and a slipping driving band presented too great a technical risk.

The UK took the alternative view, and applied the slipping driving band technique to the long rod penetrator to decouple it from the spin given to it by a rifled barrel. This left HESH, smoke, smoke and canister available; if HESH is available, then there is no requirement for a separate HE round. HEAT is not necessarily ruled out, nor indeed is APDS if a radical change in armour arrays defeats APFSDS.

The argument thus resolves itself into a consideration of the value of spin stabilization against fin stabilization in terms of the secondary ammunition natures available for each type of gun. These factors are presented in Table 1.

It has not been possible to give consideration to costs or training matters in this article, but the provision of suitably representative practice ammunition and its cost will be a significant factor in the choice of a new weapon system, and clearly the overall cost of ownership over the life of the weapon system will be a dominant factor, at least in the West.

Conclusions

- For a designer faced with developing a tank gun, the smoothbore gun appears a logical choice due to the relative design of the gun and its ammunition.
- The UK rifled gun is an evolutionary progressive development and allows the use of a wider range of ammunition – in particular the extremely effective HESH projectile.
- The retention of the rifled gun and spin stabilization gives greater flexibility if armour protection shows another quantum jump such as the introduction of compound armour.

In summary, despite an overwhelming world opinion in favour of the smoothbore gun, the UK has opted for a more flexible solution which does not compromise operational capability by retaining the rifled gun.

The German Territorial Army

Major J.A. English

Under the terms of the Paris Agreements of October 23, 1954, which decided the accession of the Federal Republic of Germany to NATO membership, German rearmament was limited to a maximum military strength of 500 000 men and 12 divisions, the latter to be placed under NATO integrated command in war. Today's modern *Bundeswehr* is thus clearly conceived as an armed force in an alliance.

The Federal Republic, only allowed by its 1949 Basic Law or Constitution to maintain a defensive posture, has accordingly adopted a military policy of total defence, focussing upon defensive operations on home territory in the event of aggression. In defending Central Europe against an attack by the Warsaw Pact, of course, the entire Federal Republic would be included in the combat zone. Unfortunately, since Germany provides 50 per cent of all NATO land forces earmarked for forward deployment in this region, total defence has received less than its fair share of attention. The role of the German Territorial Army, in particular, is not well understood and it consequently tends to be underestimated; yet, in the army of the *Bundeswehr* it has vital tasks to perform.

Simply put, German total or overall defence includes a civil as well as a military dimension. While military defence in the North Atlantic Alliance aims to protect the way of life and territory of the Federal Republic from outside threat, civil defence aim to ensure the proper functioning of both state and government, the protection and supply of the civilian population, and the adequate support of the field forces. NATO-conducted defence, of course, also takes the civil consideration into account, though it tends to concentrate upon the operations of assigned field forces. Those portions of the total defence that are not covered by NATO, however, fall into the category of German national defence, the civil aspects of which are the concern of the Federal Ministry of the Interior. The military aspects of national defence are addressed by several German agencies and commands, especially the Territorial Army, which in war would represent the vital interests of the German population to NATO commanders.

Originally, the Territorial Army was responsible for purely national functions such as personnel replacement, medical, and logistic support for NATO-assigned German field forces. To this were later added other tasks, which, in the understanding of all allied nations, would be best performed by the host nation upon whose territory NATO forces were operating. The major Territorial Army responsibility in this regard is that of maintaining freedom of operation for NATO forces throughout the combat zone. The type

and scope of such support will, of course, differ in importance and degree of obligation within the various components of the combat zone. Tasks associated with the maintenance of freedom of operation are rear area security, military movement control, area damage control, river crossing operations, NBC reconnaissance and decontamination, and psychological defence. More specifically, the current responsibilities of the German Territorial Army can be enumerated as follows:

Rear Area Security. In the Rear Combat Zone (RCZ) the Territorial Army will play the main role in ensuring security, to include area and vulnerable-point-defence, damage control, and NBC defence. Territorial commanders will also be responsible for land-organization in the RCZ on behalf of NATO commanders concerned, i.e. allocation of areas to the forces of all allies in detail and integrating them in the overall system of RCZ security. For this reason it is critical that they be notified early of all movements into, out of, or within the RCZ. It is in the maintenance of freedom of manoeuvre – a host nation responsibility – that the close interrelation of national and NATO tasks becomes evident. While in the Forward Combat Zone (essentially corps areas) NATO commanders assume responsibility, Territorial Army commanders in the RCZ take action over and above their national obligations by fulfilling some of the tasks for which NATO is responsible.

Movement Control. As not all NATO forces are stationed in the vicinity of their areas of operation, some will have to be brought forward from the western parts of the Federal Republic, others from their home countries, and still others from overseas. Territorial Army headquarters will therefore co-ordinate their initial movements within the Federal

The German Territorial Army is equipped with main battle tanks, APCs, anti-tank missile systems and artillery weapons

Republic, making allowance for the requirements of the civil population. In order to ensure the swift crossing of the numerous water obstacles in West Germany, Territorial Army ferries and bridging equipment will be employed as necessary. Engineer forces will also be tasked to maintain the military roads in the Rear Combat Zone, to secure highly threatened points along such roads, and render support in movement control and traffic regulation.

Logistic Support. German field forces are fully dependent for logistic back-up upon a system of installations augmented by mobile units, the major portion of which is operated by the Territorial Army. Under NATO Standardization Agreement 2135, however, allied units requiring mutual logistic support will also be permitted to draw from this system. Considerable logistic support to both German and allied forces will also be provided from civilian resources, access to which is again through the Territorial Army.

Civil-Military Cooperation. In peacetime the Territorial Army is responsible for supporting the police and the civil power in case of emergency or disaster. The high population density in the Federal Republic would, of course, call for especial protection of civilians in war. Using an area-covering information system, Territorial Army headquarters will transmit the intentions of military command authorities, provided these intentions are acceptable, to the civil agencies concerned and will, in turn, convey the wishes and requirements of such agencies to NATO command authorities. Matters like the evacuation of the civil population, the blocking of communication routes, the implementation of denial measures, the cutting of utility lines and intended mine-laying in the depth of the Combat Zone are of particular importance in this regard. The area information system will also be used to collect, transmit, and exchange important information on the military and civil security situation obtained from military and civilian sources.

Medical Support. Territorial Army hospital organization provides most of the medical support for the German Armed Forces. If required under special circumstances, however, this support will be provided to allied forces without having to obtain special authority.

Information on Local Conditions. As far as possible NATO units will familiarize themselves with their areas of operation; long distances between certain areas and the peacetime garrisons of units, plus frequent rotation of personnel, will nonetheless make this difficult. Regionally responsible Territorial Army headquarters that are familiar with local conditions will accordingly support combat forces

by providing them with information on the regional security situation; other forces and military agencies in the area, the civil situation, terrain conditions, water obstacles, the transport and road network, regional peculiarities, preparations for obstacles and denial measures, important communications, and other matters of significance that will give them operational advantages. The Territorial Army, in short, acts as mediator between military and civil interests.

While the tasks of the Territorial Army are numerous and quite troop-intensive, the Federal government has nonetheless given clear priority to its army field forces

River crossing operations are one of the tasks assigned to the Territorial Army

Levels of Cooperation

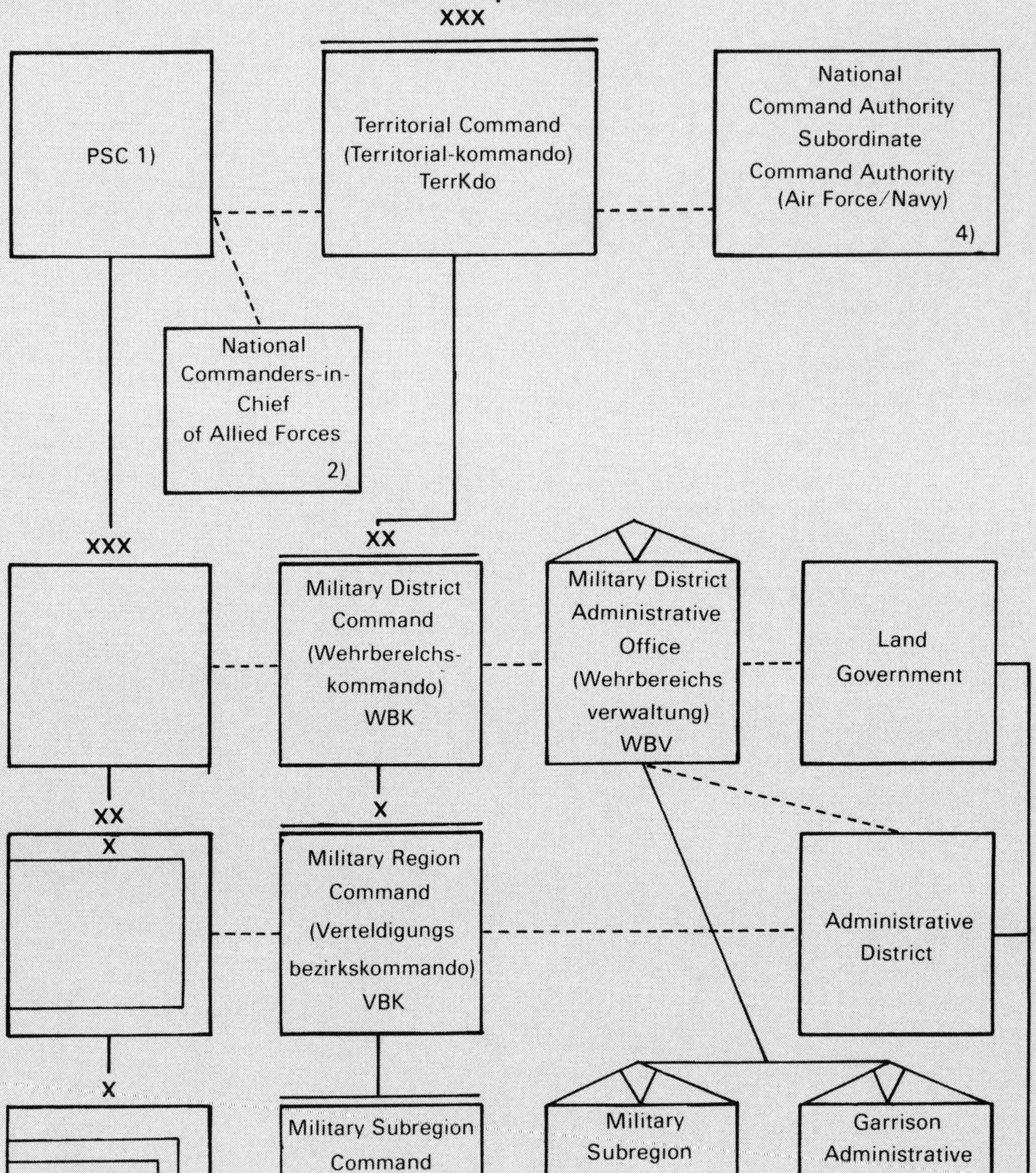

1) AAFCE, ATAF, Army Group, BALTAP, BERNOSEA, LANDJUT

2) BAOR, CFE, FBA, FFA, RAFG, USAFE, USAREUR

3) Independent brigade

4) HQ GAF Tactical Command, Air Force Office, GAF Support Command, GAF Northern Support Region Command, GAF Southern Support Region Command, Fleet Command, Naval Support Command

who must bear the brunt of forward defence. Out of a current peacetime establishment of approximately 340 000, the three corps and 12 divisions of the field forces account for roughly 248 000. With an additional 28 000 employed in the General Army Office, only 64 000 - most of them reserves - constitute the peacetime establishment of the Territorial Army. Within the total force concept, of course, roughly half the strength of the German army (i.e. 175 000) is made up of conscripts (though they should ideally make up but 45 per cent).

At the beginning of each quarter, about 44 000 men are called up for basic training which lasts for three months. Following this they receive one year post-basic training with an operational element. About one-fourth of the conscripts in operational formations are replaced every quarter with fresh personnel. The remaining half of army manpower (ideally it should be 55 per cent) is made up of about 35 000 regular career soldiers and 130 000 'short service' volunteers who are engaged for periods of enlistment ranging from two to 15 years.

To ensure that cadre-strength units and formations in both the field forces and the Territorial Army are fleshed-out in war, however, a substantial number of trained reservists are required. It is, of course, a central precept of German defence planning that 'in a state of defence, trained reservists must be available to augment the armed forces to wartime establishment.' Certainly, corps and divisional support units will have to rely on mobilization augmentation, which rests ultimately on the pool of trained manpower afforded by conscription. Reservists of the Standby Readiness Component, made up of selected conscripts who have just served their basic military service, and 'alert' reservists (who have been out of the army for some time) are accordingly earmarked to man the unfilled spaces.

The purpose of the former, of course, is to enable rapid augmentation of cadre-strength formations of the field forces and the Territorial Army in a period of political tension and to provide them with the capability to execute their mission. On January 24, 1975, the *Bundestag* unanimously adopted an amendment to the Compulsory Military Service Law, whereby the duration of the Standby Readiness status of reservists was extended from three months to a year. Interestingly, the Territorial Army expects to field, on mobilization, a strength of approximately 480 000 soldiers.

Area Commands

Within the Territorial Army 11 per cent of personnel belong to logistic units, a further 16 per cent to medical units, and 27 per cent are personnel replacements for the entire army. The remaining 46 per cent are split among combat forces, ranging from security platoons to mechanized home defence brigades; from engineers for river crossing support to damage control and operation of the NATO pipeline; and from military police and signal troops to NBC defence units. Structurally the organization of the Territorial Army is rooted in geography rather than tactical necessities.

It comprises three *Territorialkommando* or area commands, two major and one minor. German Territorial Northern Command (GTNC) takes in the *länder*, or provinces of Lower Saxony, North Rhine-Westphalia, and the Free Hanseatic City of Bremen. The larger German Territorial Southern Command (GTSC) encompasses the provinces of Saarland, Rhineland-Palatinate, Baden-Württemberg, Hesse, and the Free State of Bavaria. The third and smallest territorial command is based on Schleswig-Holstein and the Free and Hanseatic City of Hamburg. West Berlin is not included in German Territorial Army organization; though regarded as a Federal *land*, it remains under the Four Power Statute that governed the previous occupation of Germany.

The territorial commands are further broken down into *Wehrbereichskommando* (WBK), or military districts, geographical groupings that are essentially based on *länder* divisions. Within GTNC there are two military districts: WBK II, comprising Lower Saxony and Bremen; and WBK III, consisting of North Rhine-Westphalia. GTSC, on the other hand, consists of three military districts: WBK IV, comprising Hesse, Saarland, and the Rhineland-Palatinate; WBK V, Baden-Württemberg; and WBK VI in Bavaria. Schleswig-Holstein territorial command includes but one military district, WBK I.

The WBK themselves are sub-divided into military regions or *Verteidigungsbezirkskommando* (VBK), which are mainly based on political administrative districts (counties) or *Regierungsbezirke* and the *länder* of Saarland, Bremen, and Hamburg. In all, there are 28 VBK, each identified by a two-digit number, the first digit of which corresponds to its respective WBK (e.g. VBK 52 Karlsruhe is in WBK V, VBK 33 Munster is in WBK III, and so on). Each VBK is further sub-divided into military sub-regions or *Verteidigungskreiskommando* (VKK), of which there are roughly 80 in the Federal Republic; these are based on rural sub-districts or *Landkreise* and cities or *KreisfreieStädte*. VKKs are given three-digit numbers, the first two digits of which identify VBKs and WBKs, respectively (e.g. VKK 422 Daun is in VBK 42 Trier, which is in WBK IV).

As warfare on German territory permits the use of national civilian resources in support of NATO forces on an especially large scale, appropriate levels of coordination and cooperation have had to be established between allied military and German civil agencies. In this process Territorial Army personnel act as 'expert mediators', and a number of liaison teams have consequently been attached to each territorial headquarters so that the necessary coordination can be effected. At territorial command level coordination is achieved with NATO Principal Subordinate Commands such as Central Army Group or Northern Army Group, and allied national headquarters such as United States Army Europe, British Army of the Rhine, and Canadian Forces Europe. The appropriate level of cooperation for WBKs is field army corps and *länder* government authorities. For VBK the equivalent level is NATO division or independent brigade and *Regierungsbezirke* which exercise administrative control over rural sub-districts *(Landkreise)* and cities *(kreisfreieStädt)*. At VKK level coordination is mainly effected with NATO brigades and below and with Territorial Army recruiting and administrative agencies. It is worth noting, however, that maximum flexibility is required in working with field forces since German Territorial Army geographic divisions do not always fit exactly with NATO tactical dispositions. Fortunately, GTNC and GTSC cover roughly the same areas, respectively, as do Northern Army Group and Central Army Group.

Keeping reservists trained to the required level is a continuing problem

From a command and control viewpoint it should be mentioned that Territorial Army headquarters at all levels are only manned to a limited extent in peacetime. Their respective establishments, however, include regular force (including general staff officers), 'short service', conscript, and reserve personnel, and each will in war possess numbers of headquarters troops such as engineers, signallers, medics, and police. On the outbreak of hostilities, of course the peacetime establishments of territorial headquarters would be largely augmented and combat commands or *Verfügungstruppenkommando* (VTK) would also be formed. The latter could be placed under WBK control, or, alternatively, operate independently under territorial commands. The five slated for activation in war are: VTK 44 in WBK IV; VTK 45 in WBK V; VTK 46 in WBK VI; VTK 42 in WBK II; VTK 43 in WBK III; and VTK 41 in Schleswig-Holstein territorial command (WBK I).

As previously indicated, Territorial Army headquarters also have under their command units in various force mixes as required for their specific tasks. Essentially, these are divided into security and manoeuvre troops: the former armed with mainly infantry weapons for the protection of military targets and regions; and the latter, consisting of heavily mechanized home defence brigades armed with tanks, artillery, and anti-tank weapons, designed to repel enemy air or sea landings; and to combat sabotage squads operating behind friendly force lines. Both security and manoeuvre elements – the home defence component – are currently being reorganized in accordance with Army Structure Number 4, which is expected to be fully implemented by 1985.

The security troops will include 45 motorized infantry battalions organized in 15 home defence regiments to be employed in area defence, eight in GTSC, five in GTNC, and two in Schleswig-Holstein, plus 150 home defence companies and 300 security platoons for vital point protection in the rear area. In peacetime they will also be devised as equipment holding units.

As regards manoeuvre elements, the organizational structure and equipment of six home defence brigades is presently being adapted to that of field force armoured infantry brigades; like the latter, they will comprise four manoeuvre battalions and one artillery battalion. The peacetime manning level of two of these brigades will be at 85 per cent of war establishment, two will be at 65 per cent, and two will be at 52 per cent. Six additional home defence brigades equipped with heavy weapons are planned; in peacetime, however, they will be devised as equipment holding units.

Four of the aforementioned home defence brigades are located in GTNC: HDB 52 and HDB 62 with WBK II; and HDB 53 and HDB 63 with WBK III (again, numbers are significant; the second digit identifying WBK, and the first the status of the unit – the figure 5 indicating 'cadre-strength', and the figure 6 'equipment holding'). Within GTSC there are six such home defence brigades: HDB 54 and HDB 64 with WBK IV; HDB 55 and HDB 65 with WBK V; and HDB 56 and HDB 66 with WBK VI. HDB 51 and HDB 61 are located in Schleswig-Holstein territorial command (WBK I).

The heavy weapons needed to raise the combat power of home defence forces will become available by

degrees. Weapons of the German field forces replaced in the course of modernization will, after partial retrofit, be incorporated into the Territorial Army arsenal. Upgunning the M-48 main battle tank with the 105 mm armament of the Leopard 1, for example, should greatly enhance the firepower and anti-armour capability of the home defence forces. Upon completion of the Leopard 2 deployment, the German army will have 4887 main battle tanks in its units and reserve stocks. Through judicious use of existing equipment and armaments the Germans hope to avoid additional costly procurement of entirely new major weapons systems. This approach is definitely sensible as reserve forces are highly expensive to retain in peacetime. Not only does material have to be procured, stored, and maintained, but reservists themselves have to be trained and continually retrained to keep them fit for tasks which armed forces like the German Territorial Army have to undertake.

Although the German Territorial Army has the ancillary function of acting to support and set free NATO forces for forward defence, it should be recognized that this is an extremely critical function. How well NATO troops fight in the forward areas will no doubt directly reflect the effectiveness of the civil-military effort behind them. The formidable air and helicopter-borne power that Warsaw Pact forces are capable of projecting into NATO rear areas is, of course, a real threat which must be addressed.

Fortunately the Territorial Army permits maximum exploitation of those advantages inherent to the waging of war on home territory. As the prescient British military theorist, Major Tom Wintringham, pointed out years ago:

> The answer to attack in depth is the defence in depth, and this defence must cover the whole area of the nation under attack. Yet we know that every army lacks sufficient manpower to defend at one time every foot of ground against the modern form of attack. If the rear is soft, it is always especially vulnerable.

The aim of the German Territorial Army is to ensure that it is not.

Pause in manoeuvres for German territorials

Bibliography

White Paper 1979: The Security of the Federal Republic of Germany and the Development of the Federal Armed Forces. Bonn: Federal Ministry of Defence, 1979.

Burandt, Lt. Gen. Eberhard. 'Indispensable Partner', *NATO's Fifteen Nations* (Special Issue 2, 1981), 54-60.

Information: Federal Republic of Germany Armed Forces Bonn: Press and Information Office, 1979.

Federal Armed Forces Facts and Figures. Bonn: Federal Ministry of Defence, 1981.

Philipp, Udo 'NATO Strategy Under Discussion in Bonn', *International Defence Review* (No 9, 1980), 1367-1371.

Interview with Major Justus Graebner, German Army General Staff, War Plans, G-3. Central Army Group Headquarters.

78

Central Army Group

Pillar of Nato Defence

Major J.A. English

In General Sir John Hackett's gripping book *The Third World War*, the point is quite strongly made that in spite of the great importance of NATO's flanks, the most critical area for the Alliance on land remains the Central Region of Allied Command Europe.[1] According to intelligence estimates, the Warsaw Pact has earmarked up to 101 divisions for possible employment against Central Europe, of which at least 85 would face Central Region. A total of 58 divisions with 19 000 main battle tanks are currently stationed in East Germany, Czechoslovakia, and Poland; this force includes 27 Soviet divisions, 20 of them forming the Group of Soviet Forces Germany (GSFG).

The odds facing CENTAG are imposing, but not insurmountable

The Southern Group of Forces could go against CENTAG

Another 33 combat ready divisions with 8500 main battle tanks are capable of moving forward in a matter of days from the Baltic, Belorussian, and Carpathian Military Districts located in the western reaches of the Soviet Union. Finally, ten divisions (including the Soviet Southern Group of Forces (SGF) of four divisions and 2700 main battle tanks stationed in Hungary could conceivably be launched against Central rather than Southern Europe if the situation warranted.[2]

Central Region, or Central European Command as it is sometimes termed[3], contains the industrial heartland of Western Europe; it encompasses all territory within the Benelux nations and the Federal Republic of Germany south of the Elbe River. The Commander-in-Chief, Central Region (CINCENT), formerly a French officer but since 1966 a German, is charged with the

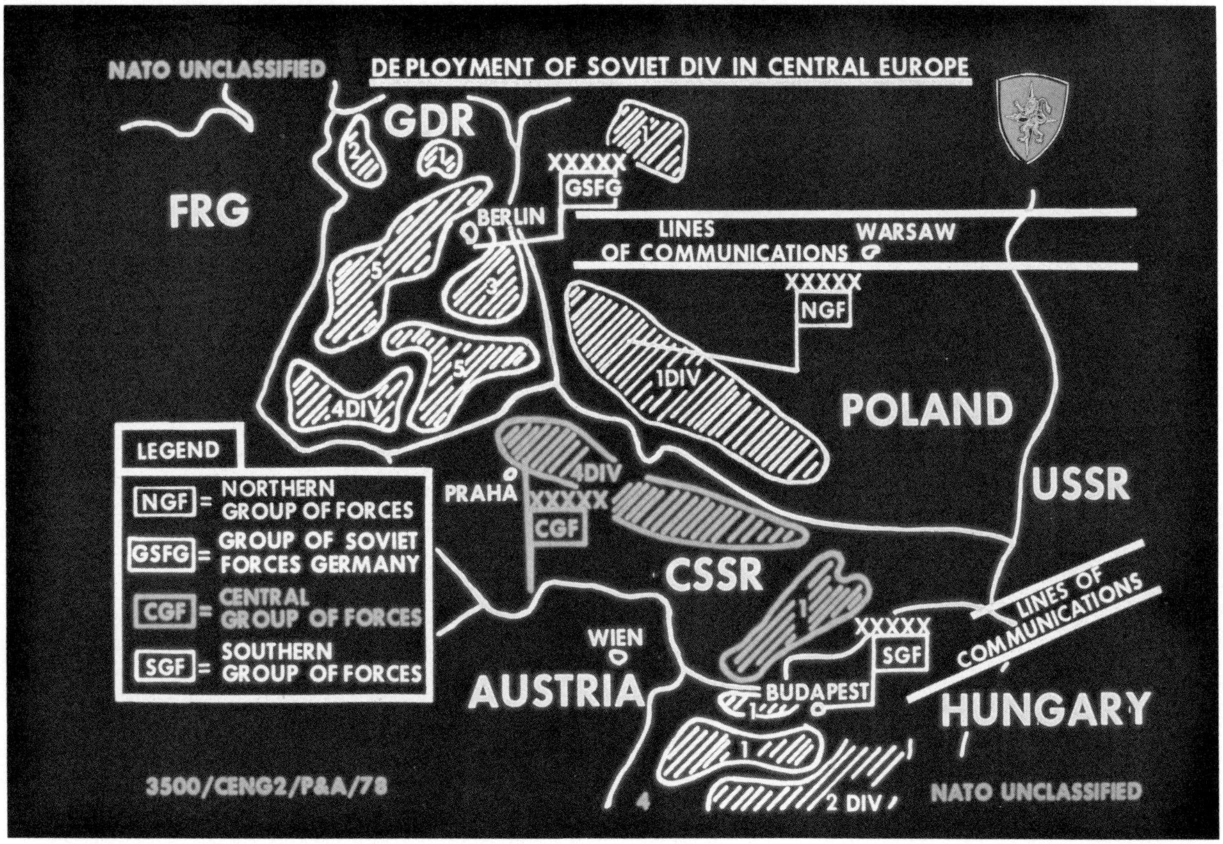

defence of this region and command in war of all Allied Forces Central Europe (AFCENT) – currently the greatest concentration of Allied ground and air forces in NATO. The Principal Subordinate Commands of AFCENT are Central Army Group (CENTAG), Northern Army Group (NORTHAG), and Allied Air Forces Central Europe (AAFCE). The last was established in 1974 with an overall US commander and separate headquarters to direct the integrated and more flexible employment of Central Region air resources in accordance with CINCENT's directives. Both army groups are supported by AAFCE tactical air forces: Second Allied Tactical Air Force (2ATAF) associated with NORTHAG; and Fourth Allied Tactical Air Force (4ATAF) associated with CENTAG.[4]

Just as NORTHAG has since its inception in 1952 been commanded by the incumbent Commander-in-Chief, British Army of the Rhine, CENTAG has to date been commanded by the Commander-in-Chief, United States Army Europe (USAEUR). In fact, 'Central Army Headquarters,' as it was first known to part-time US Army NATO defence planners in 1952, was actually part of the operations office of Headquarters, USAEUR. The following year, a full time CENTAG planning group of French and American officers was established. Augmented by German officers on activation of the *Bundeswehr* in January 1956, the planning group eventually became a provisional headquarters in 1959 and an integrated NATO headquarters in October 1960.

On the withdrawal of the French from military integration within NATO in 1966, CENTAG became a bi-national formation until 1970 when 4 Canadian Mechanized Brigade Group (4CMBG) departed NORTHAG for CENTAG and collocated with Canadian Forces Europe in the south-western corner of the Federal Republic. Today the staff of Headquarters CENTAG, relocated since 1980 in Campbell Barracks,

Heidelberg, is composed of about 48 per cent American, 48 per cent German, and four per cent Canadian in rough approximation of national strength contributions to CENTAG field forces.[5] In peacetime this 500-man tri-national headquarters (including a 200-man support command) is primarily involved in contingency war planning and the conduct of readiness exercises. In war, however, it would control all American, German, and Canadian field forces within the CENTAG sector.

The CENTAG sector of the Central Region runs roughly from near Kassel in the north, at the junction with I Belgian Corps on the right of NORTHAG, to the Austrian frontier south of Munich. With a land mass of about 93 208 sq miles (150 000 km^2), this area represents approximately 60 per cent of the total territory of the Federal Republic. In addition to many important economic centres, factories, farming areas, land routes, and waterways, the sector also possesses in its 30 million inhabitants about half the population of West Germany.[6] While the primary mission of CENTAG is to deter war in this sector, its field forces have the far more awesome task, in the event deterrence fails, of defending southern Germany from hostile incursion.

The fact that the Rhine River between Wiesbaden and Karlsruhe is but 93 miles (150 km) from the East German border is of particular concern in this regard, since such a geographic shortcut could well invite a Warsaw Pact attack with the aim of cutting the Federal Republic in two and separating CENTAG from NORTHAG. Any seizure of bridgeheads over the Rhine would additionally permit enemy forces a choice of militarily advantageous options: by consolidating along the east bank of the Rhine they could defend from a very favourable position against Allied counter

CENTAG and 4ATAF are collocated in Campbell Barracks, Heidelberg

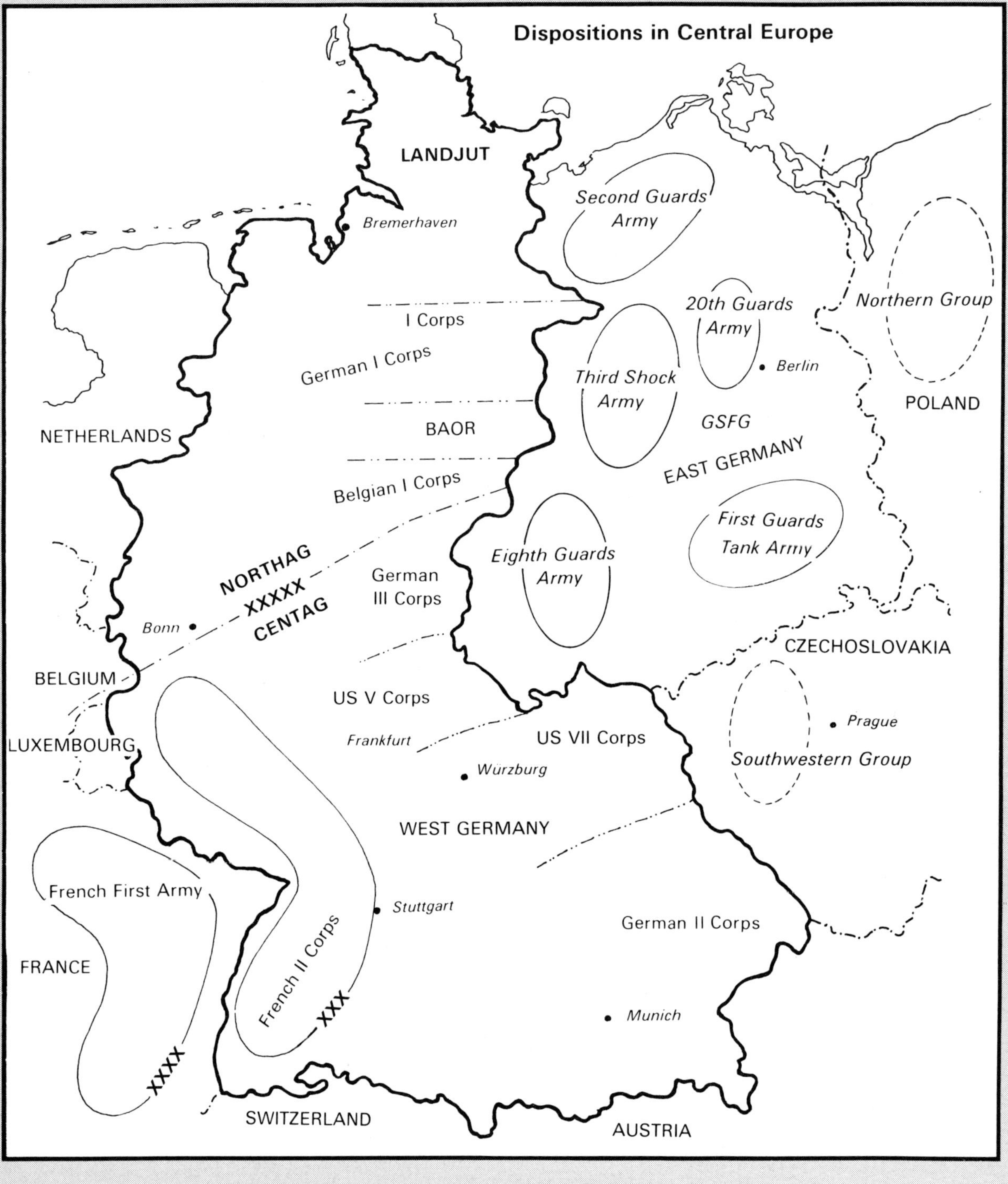
Dispositions in Central Europe
LANDJUT
Bremerhaven
Second Guards Army
Northern Group
20th Guards Army
I Corps
German I Corps
Third Shock Army
Berlin
POLAND
GSFG
NETHERLANDS
BAOR
EAST GERMANY
Belgian I Corps
First Guards Tank Army
NORTHAG
XXXXX
CENTAG
German III Corps
Eighth Guards Army
Bonn
CZECHOSLOVAKIA
BELGIUM
US V Corps
Prague
LUXEMBOURG
Frankfurt
US VII Corps
Southwestern Group
Wurzburg
WEST GERMANY
French First Army
Stuttgart
French II Corps
German II Corps
FRANCE
XXX
Munich
XXXX
SWITZERLAND
AUSTRIA

attacks; or, alternatively, they could use the bridgeheads as bases for continuing a western offensive. In any event, the destruction of important industrial complexes along the Rhine and the psychological impact of a successful enemy attack to the Rhine would be extremely damaging to NATO.[7]

Given the assessment that force ratios on the CENTAG front favour the Warsaw Pact by 3:1 in tanks, 5:1 in artillery, and 3:1 in other land combat systems,[8] CENTAG forces obviously face challenging, though not necessarily insurmountable, odds. Fortunately, much of the eastern portion of the CENTAG sector is characterized by ground that is more favourable to defence than offence.[9] Heavily wooded hilly features like the Kaufungerwald Knullgebirge, the Rhön-Spessart mountain chain, the Frankenwald, Fichtelgebirge, Oberpfälzerwald, and the Bayerischerwald are, in fact, natural hindrances to rapid enemy movement. Such obstacles tend, moreover, to canalize an advancing enemy along more open but less numerous approaches that have, without exception, been subjected to detailed examination and study by appropriate levels of CENTAG field forces.

(Left) Allied and Soviet Dispositions in Europe

Major conurbations such as Nürenberg, Munich, the Rhine-Main complex, and even the urban sprawl developing on the line Frankfurt-Karlsruhe, would additionally limit an attacking enemy's freedom of movement.[10] In short, the current and rapidly growing urbanization of southern Germany continues to present CENTAG defenders with a certain edge. Considering the greatly increased power with which modern weaponry has graced the defence, Clausewitz's 'intrinsically stronger' form of combat,[11] such topographic features as exist in southern Germany may well provide CENTAG with much more than a passing advantage.

Field-force

It is, of course, also of relative significance that of the 6500 main battle tanks and 28 in-place divisions disposed by NATO[12] throughout the length of the Federal Republic from Denmark to Austria, 12 of the latter belong to the CENTAG order of battle. Together with 4CMBG and supporting troops, these five strong armoured and seven mechanized infantry divisions

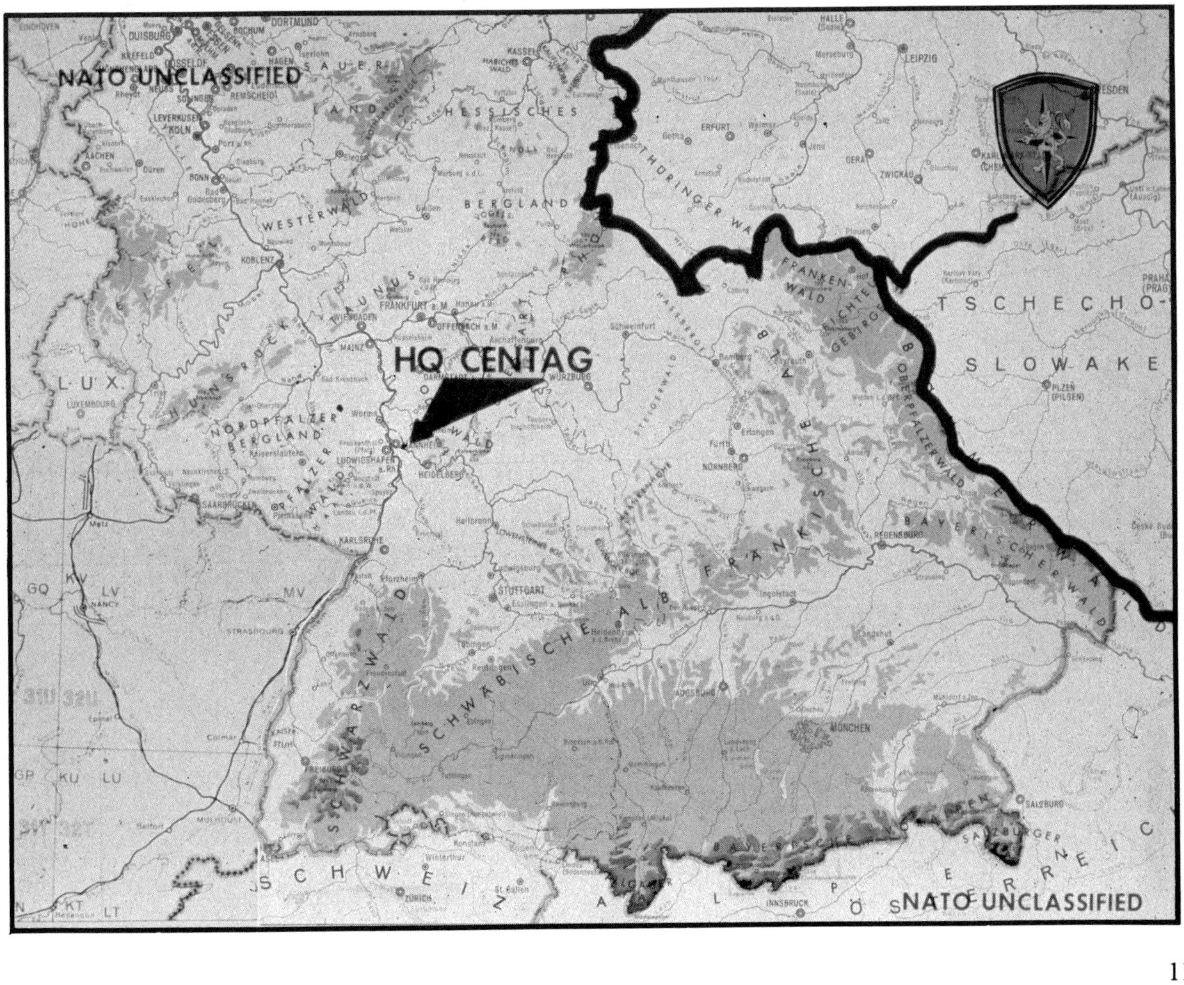

(Below) The CENTAG sector contains 60 per cent of the territory and half the population of the Federal Republic

constitute a CENTAG field force of more than 300 000 soldiers (compared to 200 000 in NORTHAG).[13] Specifically, they are deployed from north to south as follows:

III German Corps comprising 2nd Panzergrenadier and 5th Panzer Divisions and Airborne Brigade, 26.

V US Corps comprising the 8th Mechanized Infantry and 3rd Armoured Divisions the 11th Armored Cavalry Regiment, and the 4th Brigade of the 4th Mechanized Infantry Division.

VII US Corps comprising 12 (German) Panzer Division, the 3rd Mechanized Infantry and 1st Armored Divisions, the 2nd Armored Cavalry Regiment, and one brigade of the 1st Mechanized Infantry Division (Forward). The remainder of the 1st Mechanized Infantry Division and the 3rd Armored Cavalry Regiment are slated to be flown from the US as part of a 'Reforger' reinforcement package.

II German Corps comprising 4th Panzergrenadier, 10th Panzer, and 1st Mountain Divisions, plus Airborne Brigade 25 and Headquarters, 9th Airborne Division.[14]

Backing up CENTAG field forces is the German Territorial Army Southern Command (GTSC). Al-

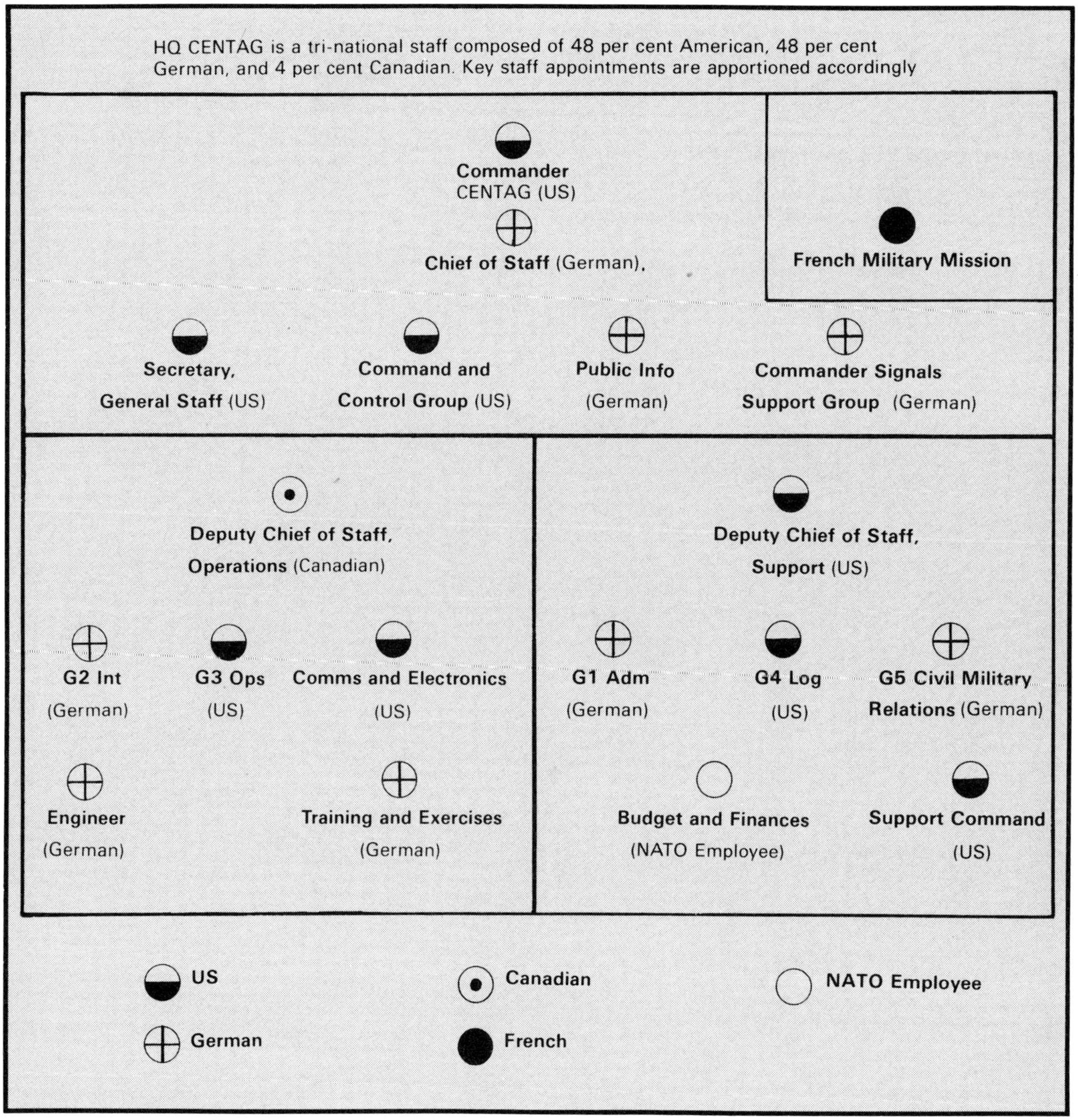

though it will remain under national command in war, GTSC is responsible for maintaining freedom of operations in the rear combat zone of the CENTAG sector. It is specifically responsible for the planning and supervision of the initial deployment and later movement of all reserves and reinforcements into corps sectors.

The manning and logistical support of II and III German Corps is also a major GTSC responsibility, as is the equally critical function (in view of the Soviet airborne threat) of rear area security. Since the home defence component of the Territorial Army (ie manoeuvre and security troops) is being reorganized under 'Army Structure Number 4', significant qualitative and quantitative improvements can shortly be expected within GTSC.[15]

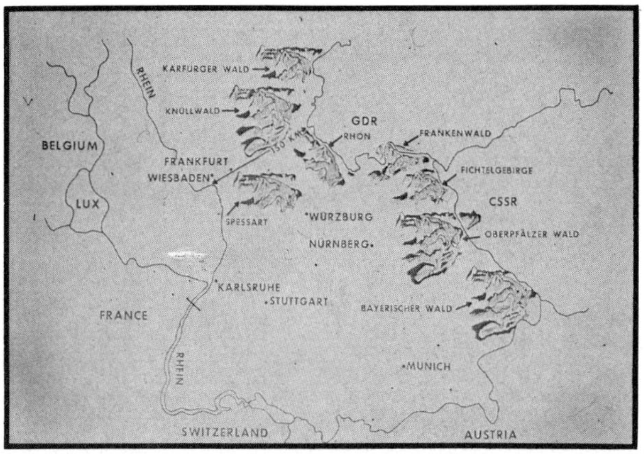

The Rhine is but 150 kilometres from the East German border

The combat effectiveness of CENTAG field forces should also shortly begin to rise dramatically as both German and US corps are now being issued with new 'Chobham-laminate' armoured[16] Leopard II and M1 General Abrams heavyweight tanks, assessed as 'the two most advanced battle tanks in the West.[17] American forces will as well undergo a tremendous modernization process as they receive 400 new equipment items over the next five years, among them AH 64 Apache and UH 60A Black Hawk helicopters, needed replacements for ageing Cobra (currently being modified) and Huey aircraft. In the meantime, German field forces will continue to take delivery of the PAH 1 anti-tank helicopter, another powerful and agile means for dealing with enemy armour.

Improved short, medium, and long range anti-armour weapons systems are also being introduced to both American and German units. The planned acquisition of modern anti-aircraft artillery systems by the US and German armies should additionally do much to enhance the air defence posture of CENTAG forces. The introduction of the new M2 General Bradley infantry fighting vehicle to American units will likewise be a most welcome qualitative improvement, as at the present moment only the German Marder can be considered the rough equal of the Soviet BMP. On completion of the equipment programmes now underway and those anticipated for the near future, CENTAG hopes to regain the traditional technological edge it formerly held over its potential enemies.[18]

Continuing force structure modernization programmes are furthermore expected to enhance the overall combat strength and battle effectiveness of CENTAG field forces. CENTAG's two German corps are currently converting to 'Army Structure Number 4', the reorganization of which will increase the number of combat units; though smaller in size, they will be more flexible on the battlefield. Interestingly too, of the 12 home defence brigades that will exist within the German Territorial Army after its reorganization is complete, six will be stationed in the CENTAG sector.

The US Army will similarly be implementing new corps and divisional organizations as part of its 'Division 86' force modernization programme. In addition to providing armoured and infantry battalions with greater hitting power, this restructuring should enhance the survivability and manoeuvre capabilities of American units.[19] Even more revolutionary, each heavy 'Division 86' will have included in its establishment an Air Cavalry Attack Brigade (ACAB), which will, to quote Maj. Gen. Louis Wagner, Commanding General of the US Armor Center, 'enable the division to fight the extremely violent, lethal and unpredictable battles of the future.'[20] When eventually fielded, AH 64 Apaches will augment the two attack helicopter battalions (of 21 AH 1S Cobras each) that will form the primary fire and manoeuvre elements of each ACAB.[21]

French Forces

No consideration of the relative strengths and weaknesses of CENTAG would be complete, however, without some reference being made to the presence of French Forces in Germany. While not specifically assigned to NATO, II French Corps is still stationed in the CENTAG sector, in close proximity to the Canadians, under terms of a Status of Forces Agreement. Organized into three divisions plus supporting troops, II French Corps constitutes a formidable modern fighting force of roughly 50 000 soldiers.

Though France is no longer included in the military integration of NATO, it should not be forgotten that she nonetheless remains an important member of the Atlantic Alliance. France does, moreover, cooperate with other member nations, particularly the Federal Republic, in the military field (she also maintains a French Military Mission to CENTAG). There are in existence as well, agreements between France and her NATO allies and the major NATO Commanders on the cooperation of her forces with the integrated forces of the Alliance countries in the event of war.[22] In view of this national stance, it is indeed difficult to envisage a modern rejuvenated France standing idly by during any battle for Europe. It is possible, therefore, in the words of General Frederick J. Kroesen, Commander CENTAG, 'to be optimistic that if CENTAG is required to fight, French forces will be committed to the common defence . . .'[23]

Obviously, as an alliance of nations ultimately rests on an alliance of people, the success of any CENTAG defence in the event of hostilities will probably hinge upon how well American, German, and Canadian soldiers work together. Interoperability, the ability of separate national elements to mutually benefit from their respective services and operate effectively together, is accordingly given great emphasis in CENTAG training and personnel programmes. On a grass roots personal level there are currently about 300 partner-

Leopard MBTs now being issued to the Territorials

ships within CENTAG, two thirds of them between US and German units.[24]

The independent Canadian brigade group has, moreover, convincingly demonstrated during the past decade that, language incompatibility notwithstanding, it can work as comfortably with German formations as with American. Underscoring CENTAG attempts to achieve effective force integration is the CENTAG Interoperability Program (CIP), which is subject to regular recurring review by a committee composed of officers from each major CENTAG headquarters staff branch, subordinate formations, GTSC, and USAFUR.

The basic guidelines and priority of effort for CENTAG interoperability enhancement are established as:

Each corps having the capability to command and

control an allied division, independent brigade, or GTSC home defence brigade.

Each allied division, independent brigade, or GTSC home defence brigade being able to mutually relieve each other and being capable of operating under direction of a higher headquarters of another nationality.

Each allied division and brigade being capable of counterattacking into an adjacent allied corps sector.

All adjacent brigades at intercorps boundaries being able to cooperate in defensive operations.

Although the plans and organization necessary for the deployment of CENTAG forces have evolved over nearly three decades, improvements to operational capability continue to be made. The recent collocation of 4ATAF and CENTAG headquarters in Campbell Barracks, for example, is viewed as a most progressive step toward ensuring more effective coordination of

M1 Abrams; one of the most advanced battle tanks in the West

that land/air effort considered so vital to the successful conduct of modern battle. The rehearsal of CENTAG staffs and formations in those activities for which they will be responsible in war also continues unabated; this is largely accomplished through the medium of complementary national and NATO command post exercises (CPXs) and field training exercises (FTXs). The first are intended to familiarize commanders and staffs with wartime problems, evaluate war plans, test procedures and communications, and generally examine tactical questions. The second are far more ambitious and involve actual troop participation.

In September, 1979, for the first time in NATO history, Headquarters CENTAG conducted a major FTX, the focus of which was upon the coordination of operations between adjacent allied corps of different nations. The aim was to gain an insight into the problems CENTAG might face if an enemy attacked at a boundary between formations that did not speak the same language or use the same equipment. In this exercise, named 'Constant Enforcer', about 30 000

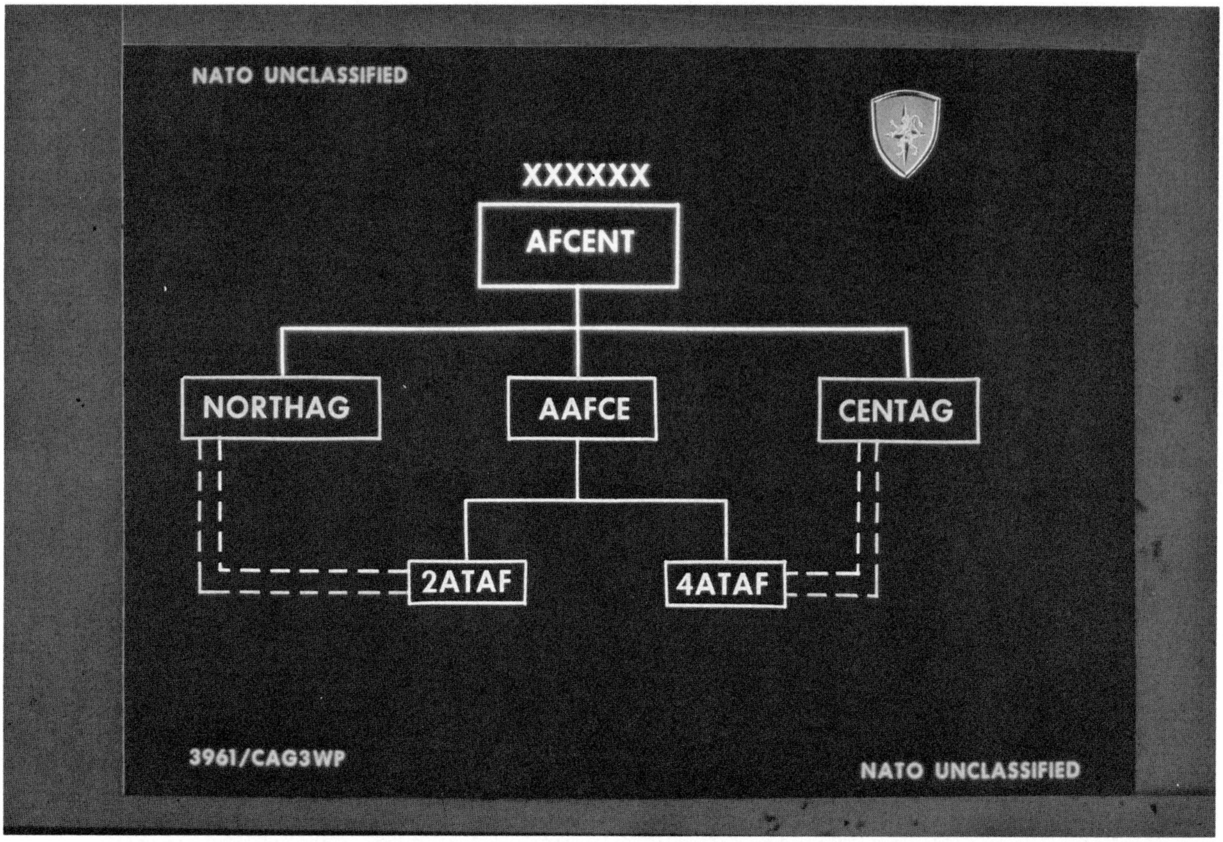

The three Principal Subordinate Commands of AFCENT are NORTHAG, AAFCE, and CENTAG

The German PAH-1 is a powerful and agile tank killer

soldiers, 2500 tracked vehicles, 300 helicopters, and 10 000 wheeled vehicles representing four NATO nations participated; over a 100 multi-national air sorties were also flown per day. Judged a great success, 'Constant Enforcer' promoted team work among CENTAG forces and demonstrated the benefits of and continued need for interoperability. It also provided some measurement of the expanding role Headquarters CENTAG has increasingly played, since its development as a separate entity, in the accomplishment of the CENTAG mission.[26]

As a stable defensive position has historically proven to be a force multiplier for the defender, CENTAG is today reasonably disposed to make any Warsaw Pact attack on southern Germany an extremely hazardous and doubtful enterprise.[27] This is not to say, however, since 'defence is inherently an infantry role',[28] that there is little requirement for additional infantry augmentation in certain of CENTAG's more rugged forward defensive areas. Of course, in view of the Warpac war fighting doctrine and the preponderant weight of Warpac armour facing CENTAG, a strong argument could also be made for additional mobile armoured reserves.

Such shortcomings notwithstanding, the fact is that with forces numbering in the neighbourhood of 300 000 troops, excluding GTSC, which can be expected to field an additional 200 000 on mobilization, CENTAG remains a pillar of NATO strength on the Central Front. Indeed, while the Warsaw Pact may wish to destroy CENTAG in detail before it can be reinforced, the chances of accomplishing this feat in timely fashion are highly risky, for the very presence of American and Canadian forces and their 'hostage' civil communities in the CENTAG sector clearly places the first line of North American defence along the intra-German border. Given planned improvements to CENTAG field force equipment and organizations, however, as well as continued government and public support, the Warsaw Pact may wisely choose not to attack at all, in which case the deterrent purpose of NATO will continue to be fulfilled.

References

1. General Sir John Hackett, *The Third World War* (Toronto: Thomas Nelson and Sons, 1979), p. 137.
2. *White Paper 1979: The Security of the Federal Republic of Germany and the Development of the Federal Armed Forces* (Bonn: Federal Ministry of Defence, 1979), p. 117; and Brig. Gen. G. Brugmann, 'Setting the Scene: The European Battlefield', *RUSI Journal* (December 1980), p. 56.
3. *The North Atlantic Treaty Organization: Facts and Figures* (Brussels: NATO Information Service,

1981), p. 108.

4. Gen. Dr. Ferdinand Senger und Etterlin, 'Defence of Central Europe: the Challenge of the 1980s', *NATO's Fifteen Nations*, Special Issue 2 (1981), p. 16; Hackett, pp. 137 and 279; and General Charles A. Gabriel, 'The Central Region Air Battle', *NATO's Fifteen Nations*, Special Issue 2 (1981); p. 27.
5. Hackett, p. 140; and General Frederick J. Kroesen, 'The Short Cut', *NATO's Fifteen Nations*, Special Issue 2 (1981), p. 40.
6. *Constant Enforcer Information Booklet* (Mannheim: CENTAG Public Information Office, 1979), p. 17; and Hackett, p. 121.
7. Kroesen, 'Short Cut', pp. 40-42.
8. Senger, p. 21; and Kroesen, 'Short Cut', p. 42.
9. As almost one third of the population and 25 per cent of the industrial capacity of the Federal Republic lies concentrated in a narrow zone 62 miles (100 km) wide west of the intra German border, any protracted battle on German soil could well result in the very destruction of what was being defended. For this reason, which is clearly stated in the 1979 White Paper, the German Federal government feels that there 'can be no alternative to forward defence', the principle by

(Right) Marder, nearest NATO equivalent to the Soviet BMP

The Cobra will be eventually replaced by the AH-64 Apache

which any battle for Germany will be conducted as far east as possible with the aim of losing as little ground as possible and keeping damage to a minimum. The 'forward defence principle' also includes recovering ground that is lost. *White Paper 1979*, p. 126; and Brugmann, p. 68.

10. Kroesen, 'Short Cut', pp. 40-42.
11. Carl von Clausewitz, *On War* (Princeton: University Press, 1976), pp. 358, 361, and 484.
12. *White Paper 1979*, p. 117.
13. *Constant Enforcer*, p. 17; and NORTHAG Public Information Sheet, September, 1980.
14. Order of battle breakdown by corps is not considered a security compromise as it can be found in any unclassified phonebook; NORTHAG Information Sheet of September 1980, also gives such detail for I Netherlands Corps.
15. The German Territorial Army has a total strength of about 40 000 in peace and 480 000 in war. Lt. Gen. Eberhard Burandt, 'Indispensable Partner',

NATO's Fifteen Nations, Special Issue 2 (1981), pp. 54-60; Kroesen, 'Short Cut', pp. 42-43; Kenneth Allard, 'Soviet Airborne Forces and Preemptive Power Projection', *Parameters*, Vol. 10, No. 4 (December, 1980), p. 42 and 44-48; and *White Paper 1979*, pp. 154-156.

16. Christopher Foss, 'Main Battle Tanks for the 1980s, '*Jane's Defence Review*, No. 1 (1980), pp. 39 and 43-45.
17. R.D.M. Furlong, 'Fireworks', *International Defense Review*, Vol. 14, No. 12 (1981), p. 1565.
18. Kroesen, 'Short Cut', p. 43, and in *Stars and Stripes*, 24 March, 1982, p. 1; *White Paper 1979*, p. 166; D.H.C. Jenkins, 'Abrams and Leopard 2: A User's View of the Heavyweights', *International Defense Review*, Vol. 14, No. 12 (1981), pp. 1657-1664; and Mark Lambert, 'The U.S, Army's Cobra Companies', *International Defense Review*, Vol. 14, No. 9 (1981), pp. 1179-1181. Three PAH-1 anti-tank regiments will be formed (Nos. 16, 36, and 26 – one for each corps), along with one company with 6 Panzergrenadier Division in Schleswig-Holstein. Mark Lambert, 'Germany's PAH-1 in Service', *International Defense Review*, Vol. 14, No. 9 (1981), p. 1171.
19. Kroesen, 'Short Cut', p. 43; and Jim Tice, 'Heavy Division Conversion Plan OK'd', *Army Times*, August 24, 1981, pp. 21-22.
20. 'AUSA '81 Part 1: Helicopters Dominate', *International Defense Review*, Vol. 15, No.1 (1982), p. 76. 21. *Ibid.*
22. *White Paper 1979*, pp. 23-24; and Senger, p. 18.
23. Kroesen, 'Short Cut', p. 43.
24. *Constant Enforcer Booklet*, p. i; and Kroesen, 'Short Cut', p. 44.
25. Kroesen, 'Short Cut', p. 44.
26. Initial Press Release, Exercise Constant Enforcer 79; *NATO Facts and Figures*, p. 111; and Kroesen, 'Short Cut', pp. 4 and 44.
27. 'Symposium: Military Strategy in Western Europe', *Armed Forces and Society*, Vol. 7, No. 1 (Fall, 1980), pp. 69-87; and Kroesen, p. 44.
28. General Frederick J. Kroesen, 'The Ultimate Weapon of War', *RUSI Journal* (December, 1980), p. 64.

Other Sources Consulted

'AUSI '81 Part 2: Weapons and Sensors', *International Defense Review*, Vol. 15, No. 2 (1981), 205-212.

Bundeswehr Facts and Figures. Bonn: Ministry of Defence, 1981.

Canby, Steven L., 'Territorial Defence in Central Europe', *Armed Forces and Society*, Vol. 7, No. 1 (Fall, 1980), pp. 51-67.

CENTAG Public Information Sheet, undated.

Gow, General Sir Michael, 'The Defence of the Northern German Plain', *NATO's Fifteen Nations*, Special Issue 2 (1981), 34-36.

Information: Federal Republic of Germany Armed Forces. Bonn: Press and Information Office, 1979.

NATO Handbook. Brussels: NATO Information Service, 1978.

'The Employment of Non-mechanized Infantry', *RUSI Journal* (December, 1980), 56-69.

The modern French Army is a formidable fighting force

New Equipment

Several very significant new weapons have entered service in the past twelve months such as the M-1 Abrams tank. Because of the high technology of modern weapons systems, research and development lead times can be over a decade. Significant prototypes have also been demonstrated which in some cases will not be in service until the 1990s. This section presents a selection of new equipment for the armies of the '80s and beyond.

The American M-1 Abrams tank is now in troop service in the USA and with US troops in Germany, in spite of several criticisms over fuel economy, track life and excessive cost

(Below) The Teledyne 'Super M60', a privately-proposed uprating of the existing American M60 main battle tank, which includes laminated armour, a fresh power plant and better fire control

(Bottom) The Kraus-Maffei 'Wildcat' twin 30 mm anti-aircraft vehicle uses Mauser cannon and a chassis based on the existing Truppenpanzer 1 armoured personnel carrier. It carries a surveillance radar and uses optronic aiming and tracking equipment

(Opposite) An American 'Roland' anti-aircraft unit fires a missile at the White Sands Proving Ground; the original proposals for adoption of this weapon by the US Army have been considerably watered down, and it is unlikely that the total number entering service will exceed about 40

(Left) Self-propelled anti-aircraft equipments continue to proliferate; this is a French proposal, using a Panhard chassis and twin 25 mm cannon

(Below) The new Swedish Army over-snow vehicle, built by Hagglund & Soner, which is to replace the well-known Volvo Bv202. It is expected that some NATO armies may well adopt this to replace their Volvos in due course

(Left) A British Army Westland 'Lynx' firing a TOW anti-tank missile during acceptance trials. This combination is now in service in BAOR

(Left centre) The Bofors RBS-70 missile has also been adapted as a defensive weapon for helicopters; it is seen here on a Westland 'Lynx'

(Left below) The Bofors 'Armad' is a combination of their existing RBS-70 anti-aircraft missile, an armoured carrier, and surveillance radar

(Below) The French 'Canon 155 TR' is about to be standardized for service; it uses an auxiliary propulsion unit to provide power for movement and for elevation, loading and other services

'Arwen 37', a 37 mm riot gun developed by the Royal Small Arms Factory, Enfield Lock. It uses a novel revolver mechanism to permit rapid firing of five shots. Ammunition for internal security has been perfected, and development is now going forward into designs of ammunition for use with infantry sections to permit anti-personnel and anti-armour use

A soldier burying a sensor for the Racal 'CLASSIC' movement detector. This will sense movement of men or vehicles and transmit it back to a central display unit, allowing a large area to bė kept under constant surveillance from a distance

(Right) The AT-4 light anti-tank launcher, together with its rocket, has been developed by FFV, the Swedish ordnance company

(Below) The French SATCP (Sol-air très courte portée) anti-aircraft missile developed by Matra. It uses a sensitive infra-red detector to lock on and track its target

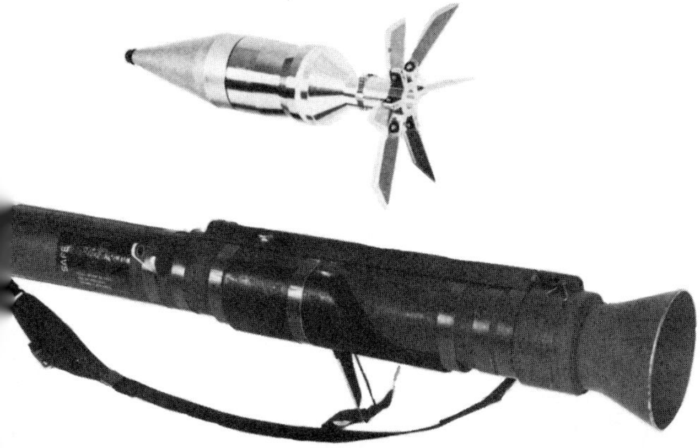

(Below) The revolutionary Heckler & Koch G-11 4.7 mm rifle which fires caseless ammunition and is scheduled for adoption by the Bundeswehr in 1990

(Bottom) Viper, the new American anti-tank launcher which will replace the existing 66 mm LAW in troop service

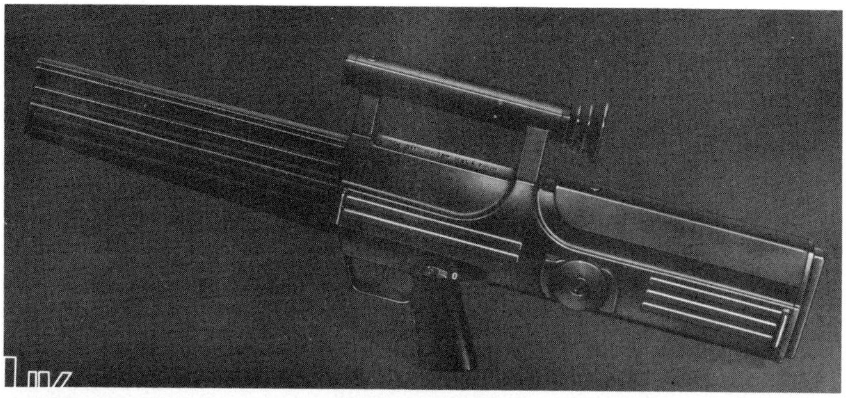

The Roles of Infantry in the Manoeuvre Battle

Richard Simpkin

The saga of tank philosophy reminds me of the story of mediaeval Irish monks locked for years in delectable disputation on the number of teeth in a horse's mouth. One day a novice, finally admitted to discussions of these mighty theological secrets, was rash enough to suggest going into the fields, finding a horse and counting its teeth. In a flash he was damned for a heretic and harried from the abbey bounds.

But at least tank philosophy has a cult object – albeit, to the regret of every self-respecting cavalryman, no longer a horse but a tin box – and this object provides a link between disputation and physical reality. 'Mechanized infantry', by contrast, stands for an idea which lacks both a doctrine and a cult object and is thus open to truly Orwellian levels of doublethink and doublespeak. Even so forceful a proponent of it as Major General Livsey, who evolved and preached the doctrine of 'active defence' when commanding Fort Benning and is now doubtless practising it with his division in 7(US) Army, is the first to admit that far too little thought has been given to this area to produce any real understanding of it. I want first, then, to dispose of three pieces of doublethink which have plagued every NATO army, except possibly the *Bundeswehr*, for at least 30 years.

First, one needs to be absolutely clear that the same men, whether marching, bundled into 'battle-taxis', mounted in Marders, hoisted in helicopters or carried around on magic carpets, *cannot do two different jobs in two different places at the same time*. Second, the fact that well trained and motivated tank crews can undergo a waiting period of several days closed down in their vehicles under NBC threat and emerge fit to fight does **not** mean that a dozen men packed like sardines into a tin box with all their equipment can do the same. The third notion, less specious but still highly misleading, is that taking an infantry battalion, organized to operate on its feet and steeped in tribal usages appropriate to that way of fighting, and packing it into mobile tin boxes qualifies it to participate in the sophisticated quickstep of the manoeuvre battle. The tank man halts between moves; the infantryman moves between positions.

Unthinkable as restrictions on money and manpower may make it, the patent fact is that the kind of battle one

The straightforward APC, such as 'Spartan' must become the standard method of transporting infantry to battle

envisages in the NATO centre may require not just two 'sets' of infantry, but three. These I shall deal with in, so to speak, increasing order of involvement in the main mobile battle.

The Infantry Battalion

Let us turn first then to the standard infantry battalion, organized and equipped for the full gamut of manpower-intensive operations worldwide – disaster relief, unarmed and armed aid to the civil power, peacekeeping, counter-insurgency, propping up the last bastions of Empire or whatever. As the tempo and scope of the air-mechanized offensive based on the doctrine of movement of masses increasingly outgrow the dimensions of the European theatre, one must constantly look at new ways to contain this threat – above all to slow it down. In these terms there seems to be an important role for the standard infantry battalion in occupying built-up areas and certain other types of terrain in sufficient strength to present a threat which will *force the attacker to move up his infantry en masse and deploy it dismounted.*

This of itself would reduce the tempo by an order of magnitude or two. But every route for the Pact's advance is liberally provided with choke points. Unless the Soviets are able to field airborne forces which are ten feet tall as well as tank crews which are five, and can spare these from their primary operations, they will

have to move this additional infantry by road, which could be a possible last straw in their movement problem.

I can recall from my school OTC days arguments raging about whether it was ethically permissible for infantry to have lorries to carry their stores - or even, dare one mention it, the men's large packs. Just as lorries became accepted and were even occasionally allowed to lift troops, so these standard battalions will inevitably come to be equipped with, or at least scaled for, armoured personnel carriers (APCs), a term which must be qualified by saying that it means a basic workhorse vehicle like M113A, FV432 or, better because lighter, FV4333 ('Stormer'), Saracen and the once despised 'Pig' soldier on in Northern Ireland to excellent effect; and the Germans may have a cost-effective class of vehicle with their wheeled *Transportpanzer* on truck chassis. But I believe that cost, the possibility of intervention in undeveloped theatres and the value of tracks in disaster relief will finally combine to outweigh the PR argument and result in a tracked vehicle.

The Mechanized Battalion

We can next turn to the conventional concept of the 'mechanized battalion', taking a look at its roles rather than philosophizing over its steeds. My studies have increasingly led me to believe that this whole concept may have been valid in the 1970s but is highly questionable for the 1980s. By the next decade, once the

revolutionary minelet and various means of massing anti-armour fire are fully available, it will be obsolete.

It is interesting, though, that a virtually identical concept has evolved in two quite different ways. Among the Anglo-Saxon prophets of position, the infantry which formed the bulk of those armies had to be given more and more mobility and protection if their participation in the contest was to remain credible, let alone feasible. At the same time a politically virtuous defensive posture combined with the traditional belief in the 'strength of the defence' in the minds of the infantry-dominated command structure to make these mechanized battalions entities in their own right, round which tactical and even operational concepts, such as Livsey's 'active defence', could be built.

Common German and Soviet armoured doctrines and experience on the Eastern Front in the Second World War convinced these armies that tanks always needed a dismountable element to fight intimately with them and to stick with them under all conditions. Yet the way the *Bundeswehr's Panzergrenadier* doctrine has developed and – far more strikingly – the great BMP controversy of the mid-1970s and the current doctrinal battle on the Soviet side have saddled both leading apostles of mobility with a mechanized infantry force which is very much an arm in its own right and makes

(Left) The German 'Marder' started out as an APC but has since come to be recognised as an MICV

(Below) The American M113 must be the most widely-used vehicle in the world stable of APCs

The Soviet BMP surprised the west by its aggressive armament of 73 mm gun and missile launcher, but it seems now to have been relegated to the role of reconnaissance vehicle

rather the same ponderous and positional noises as its Anglo-Saxon counterparts.

If one accepts this 'mechanized infantry' concept in the form it has evolved in these four major armies, I believe an infantry fighting vehicle of the Marder/M2 Bradley type is very hard to justify and that (as long as it is not yet another automotive disaster about to happen) the British MCV80 concept with its carefully planned **defensive** firepower comes much nearer the mark. In fact if one looks at concept and vehicle together, there seems to be absolutely no reason why the roles envisaged for the mechanized battalion should not be carried out by the standard infantry battalion outlined above. So to my mind the mechanized infantry concept fails one way or the other. **Either** it is out of tune with the tempo, scope and firepower pattern of the 1990s manoeuvre battle; **or** it falls very nicely within the gamut of roles of today's – or at least tomorrow's – standard infantry battalion.

On the other hand we have to face two historical facts. The primary factor in the *Wehrmacht's* defensive successes on the Eastern Front was the Germans' ability to separate the Soviet tanks from their infantry, the tanks then motoring on, often beyond artillery range, to be destroyed in detail. And the Israelis' failure to provide themselves with infantry capable of staying with their armour very nearly cost them the Yom Kippur War.

Of the three great proponents of armour, the Israelis were the only ones to fall fair and square for the heresy that tanks can operate without a dismountable element – a heresy propounded by the Salisbury Plain generals, far from dispelled by Liddell Hart, actively encouraged by de Gaulle in *Vers l'Armée de Métier* and, one suspects, avoided by Guderian mainly as a concession to **his** traditionalists. Although both their past and present armies seem less than apt at practising it, the Germans and the Soviets have never wavered in their belief in the need of tanks for *Hausinfanterie* (or 'in-house infantry'). It is ironic that the British, learning progressively the hard way throughout the Second

World War, came closest to the right answer in the 'motor battalion', bred by the cavalry dash out of the light infantry tradition of Sir John Moore and cut off in its prime 20 years later by egalitarian genetic engineering.

If the concept of 'mechanized infantry' on the lines discussed above fails because the roles fall within the spectrum of the standard infantry battalion's capabilities, that of 'mechanized infantry' as in-house infantry fails because the latter is not really infantry at all. Of the armies I have studied, the British Army still offers the best pointer to the real need with the 'assault troop' of its armoured reconnaissance regiments. This is a troop (American 'cavalry platoon') of five sections, each mounted in a light APC (formerly Saracen, now Spartan). It is primarily designed to support a reconnaissance troop of Scorpions, Scimitars or such, but can also operate as a unit in various roles.

There are two key points about these 'assault troopers' which to my mind show the way to successful in-house infantry. First, they are organic to the regiment. Theoretically at least, exchanges can take place between the assault sections and vehicle crews; certainly vehicle and section commanders are interchangeable. More important still, they all wear the same cap-badge and have inculcated into them the accepted discipline of the armoured tradition and the armoured way of living and fighting. Second, they receive special training which omits many irrelevant aspects of infantry training and throws in a number of basic field engineering and recovery skills, along with certain specialist skills such as the operation of surveillance systems based on visible light and radar.

Section size and training

Evidently, though, the assault troop as it stands will not fit the bill for the in-house infantry of the main manoeuvre force. The fundamental question is perhaps the size of the section. There seems to be little disagreement that the standard infantry section of, say, one plus ten is too large for the in-house role. This size stems on the one hand from the need to carry section weapons and ammunition for them, and on the other from the manpower-intensive nature of most positional operations.

In mobile operations (and in some types of counter-insurgency work) a large section seems to be a hindrance. Those of us who have been privileged to work with British or United States paratroops or marines appreciate that two or three fit men who really know what they are doing and leave nobody in any doubt of this can usually do the job of a full section at considerably less risk. The firepower of modern personal weapons reduces the need for section weapons, and the fire support available from vehicle-mounted weapons carries this trend further. In various books and articles I have consistently suggested a section of one plus six for the in-house role and this has gone unchallenged.

The training of these men needs to cover four separate groups of skills and must therefore be purpose-designed with great care. First, the small-crewed armoured vehicle weapon platforms of the future will need supporting manpower on the spot; if contamination prevents these crews dismounting (because of

(Right) Primitive as it may be, the Soviet BTR still has its attractions for many armies, simplicity and robustness being among them

(Below) The British MCV-80 by GKN-Sankey will be armed with a 25 mm cannon and will be the basic vehicle for a number of variants

the impossibility of decontaminating the crew compartment) this need is redoubled. Prominent in this 'chores' group are assistance with replenishment, track-bashing and battlefield recovery.

The second group consists of basic field engineering skills. If one thing stands out more clearly than another, it is that the future manoeuvre battle is not going to wait for the sappers. At every tactical level, the whole concept of 'instant preparation' of defensive positions calls for men on the spot who can carry out simple obstacle improvement and other forms of local mobility denial.

The third aspect of training is dismounted combat. Even here, the requirement matches what used to be called scouting or skirmishing rather than conventional infantry training. Almost by definition, these men are going to do most of their fighting in close country. They must be able to move fast and unobtrusively; and tempo dictates that the use and improvement of natural cover from view and fire will be more important than ritual digging. In a word, they need to learn about fieldcraft, shooting fast from the hip and other forms of instant individual reaction.

The fourth group of skills, which should in my view be limited to in-house infantry, is the bringing of effective fire to bear with any vehicle-mounted weapons in the section compartment (such as Marder's rear machine gun) and with personal weapons using periscopes and NBC-proof weapon ports. This training programme is a topic in its own right, but I believe this very brief outline brings out how radically it differs rather widely from normal infantry training.

Tank-infantry balance

The next aspects to be considered before turning to the question of a mount for these men are organizational – the 'tank-infantry' balance, effective integration and flexibility. As long as the main battle tank concept reigned and this vehicle mounted an anti-armour weapon system far outweighing in importance all others put together, a tank was a tank was a tank; and it was fairly simple to envisage the tank-infantry balance at any level from tank/section upwards. With (as I write) the Franco-German MBT project seemingly headed

for the economic rocks on which all previous collaborative tank projects have foundered, the Americans and the Swedes steering towards a 'hi/lo' profile (of tank destroyer and fire support tank) and the hermaphrodite Merkava well into its second stage of development, the 'square' or tactically balanced manoeuvre force of the future is likely to have a numerical preponderance of weapon platforms.

On top of this, the revolutionary massing of anti-armour firepower made possible by the attack helicopter, indirect anti-armour weapon systems (the so-called PGMs) and the minelet will make a force 'tank-heavy' (or rather *firepower*-heavy) without actually increasing the number of close-combat anti-armour weapon systems. So the 'tank-infantry balance' of a battle group or formation will come to depend less on the actual number of 'tanks' (or the equivalent) and infantry sections than on the artillery and rotary and fixed-wing support allocated to it.

Marching with this factor is another, different in kind but at least equal in importance. The Anglo-American prophets of position have been programmed for as long as I can remember on the elliptical routine: 'Defence - positional - infantry; attack - mobile - tanks.' There is mounting evidence that this attitude is being seriously questioned. As photographs of recent parades show, the Israelis have at last shed the 'tanks only' heresy and are well into battle-taxis. This looks like being only a short-lived phase, particularly as Merkava allows them to

(Left) The French have few doubts about wheeled vehicles, as their Renault VAB models show

(Below) Wheeled APCs, such as this Soviet BTR-60, have many adherents in Warsaw Pact armies, but the west are undecided as to their merits

trade off ammunition for the privilege of carrying a small in-house section in the rear compartment.

The Germans have never been in any doubt that the key role of in-house infantry (and other forms of support) was to help tanks get forward. And despite their wrangling about higher tactical and operational doctrine, the Soviets have steadily moved towards the balanced tank-infantry team, with increasingly massive artillery support, at the lower levels. The upshot of all this is agreement on the view that a balanced tank-infantry team with the same scale of close support is needed for defence and attack alike on most kinds of ground – in other words for the most frequent and most important types of operation.

So far, though, none of these five armies has carried this view to its logical conclusion in the shape of composite tank-infantry units – a step the French and the Swedes took quite a while back with battalions with two companies each of tanks and mechanized infantry. Once the Rubicon of the composite battalion is crossed, the trend will inevitably be towards integration at company and finally at platoon level. What actually prevents other armies from following suit is the gut reaction of arms tradition. (Fascinatingly, although recommended by Fort Knox and other authoritative agencies, the composite battalion was finally rejected for the US Army's 1986 reorganization 'because the Army is not yet ready for it.')

The Canadian Army has adopted the 'Grizzly', seen here in Norway. It is basically a Swiss Mowag vehicle with an American Cadillac Gage turret

A doubtful concept

But there are two rational arguments against the composite unit. One is that, the further down the organization integration proceeds, the more serious the loss of flexibility. Given the traditional Anglo-Saxon approach, this argument is unanswerable. But I believe I have illustrated above that what 'tank-infantry balance' is really about is becoming less dependent both on the actual proportions of weapon platforms and infantry vehicles and on the ability to vary them. By the 1990s, the need will be either for a balanced, close-knit team of direct-fire weapon platforms and dismountable elements, or for some quite differently structured force.

The second set of arguments against organic integration concerns training and logistics – and to no small extent available peacetime accommodation. As long as one has Leopard 2 or M1 Abrams and Marder or M2 Bradley, this case too is unshakeable. So this is the point at which to have the argument about a mount for the in-house infantry.

Looking at my years of involvement with the MICV (as it then was) and at the way things have gone since, I have reached the rather cynical conclusion that no

sound solution for the mechanized infantry's vehicle has been found because the mechanized infantry concept is itself, at root, unsound. The battle-taxi solution optimized in M113A1 had quite a lot going for it because it stood for a tactical concept which, despite its limitations, was at least clear-cut and realistic and because it provided a durable, reasonably cheap and highly versatile workhorse hull. (Because of the shortcomings of FV432, the MCV80 family may possibly make sense in these terms.)

I have not yet seen a full set of figures for M2 Bradley, but the real cost of the (cancelled) XM723 MICV was four times that of M113A1, while Marder cost six times as much as M113A1 and not a great deal less than the Leopard 1 tank. On the Soviet side, the BMP heyday was short-lived, most likely because of its low level of protection and the characteristics of its 'gun' (in fact a rocket-launcher). Now we see it being used in Afghanistan and probably becoming a medium reconnaissance vehicle, while the motor rifle battalions facing NATO have largely been re-equipped with the seemingly obsolescent MTLB.

On the other hand, with tanks like Chieftain, M60, Leopard 2 and M1 *General Abrams* around and with Challenger in view, the idea of an infantry fighting vehicle based on the MBT was not just mind-boggling but purse-emptying. This is why I regard the Swedish test vehicle which put the 105 mm tank gun on the Marder hull as a symbol of revolution regardless of its specific merits or demerits. There is no doubt whatever that, certainly if the tank role came to be filled by a pair of vehicles and very possibly without this step, a Class 40 family of vehicles for the main manoeuvre force will become feasible by the 1990s. With a section of one plus six, this opens the way to an infantry fighting vehicle in

Artist's impression of the IFV concept described by the author
The front section of the vehicle forms an integrated compound armour system containing the power train and fuel. Behind this is the crew compartment for a driver and two duplicate command stations, to either of which the weapon pod can be slaved via the on-board computer in its fire control mode. The primary vision and sighting system comes from twin multiple

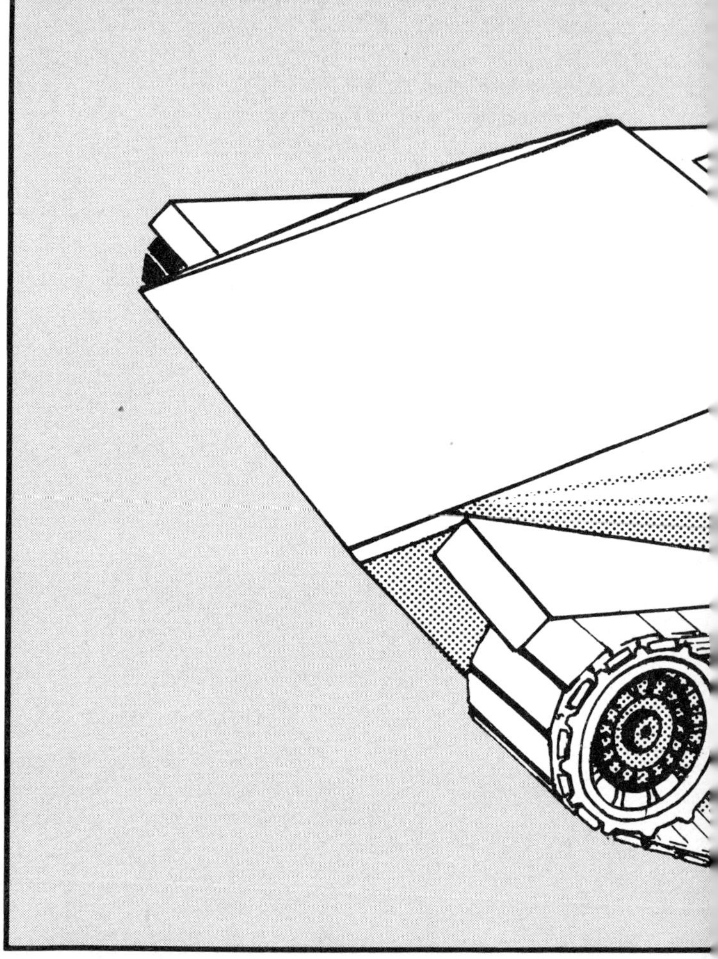

(Below) Another view of the British MCV-80, showing the roomy turret and double rear doors

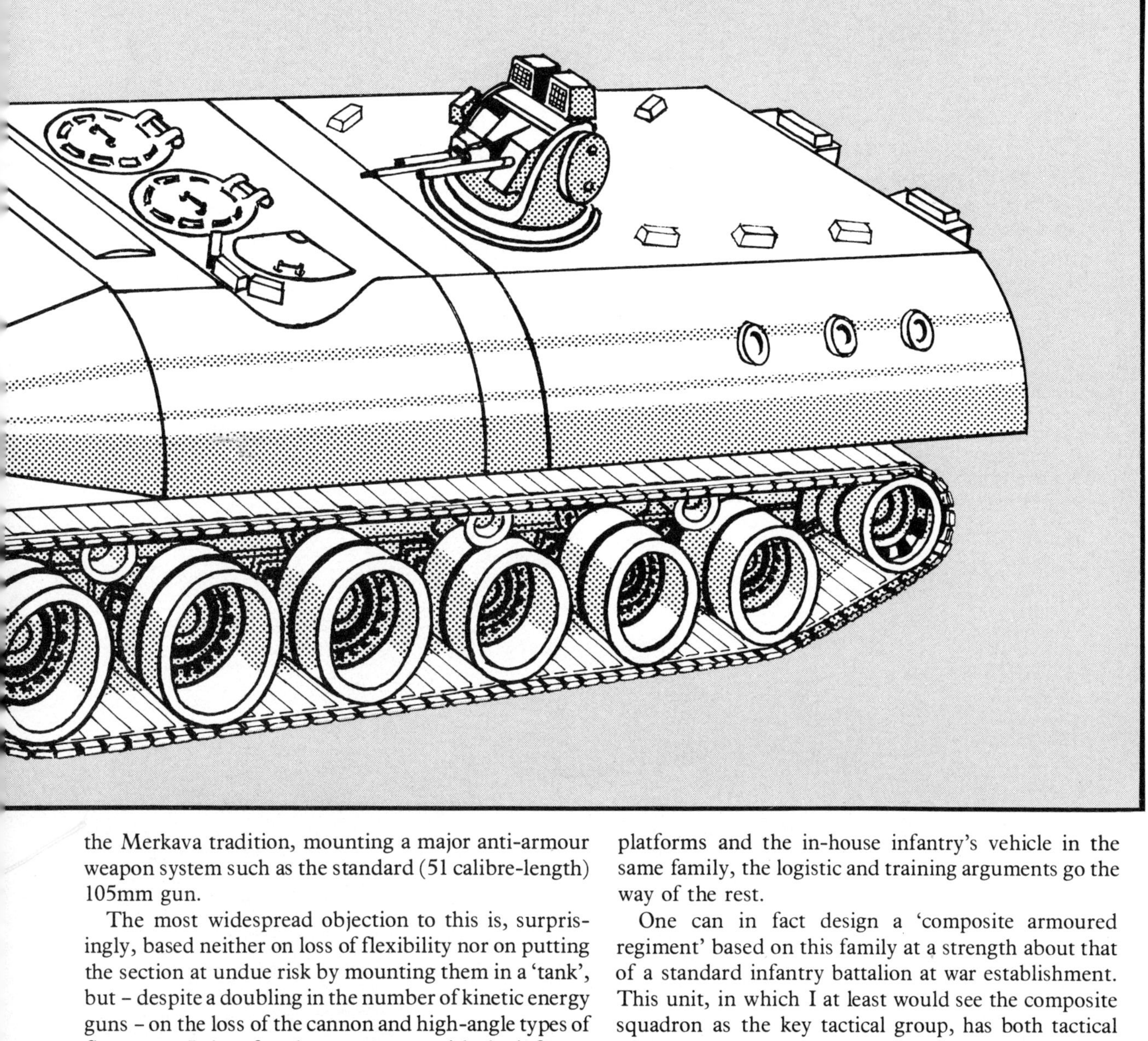

sensor heads on top of the weapon pod via an image processor to monitors in the command station. The rear compartment for six men is based on the Soviet BMP, but more roomy. The seventh position (periscope head showing behind weapon pod) is an emergency station which the section commander can occupy if forced to remount when contaminated. He normally rides in the right-hand command station, sharing surveillance and gunnery duties with the vehicle commander (centre). The rear compartment has a pull-out inner shell of boronated polyethylene; in this way it can be decontaminated or easily and cheaply renewed; or it can be replaced by liners designed for command and other specialised roles. ***(Based on artwork by Mark Irwin of Armor Magazine from the author's roughs with kind permission of the editor and artist)***

the Merkava tradition, mounting a major anti-armour weapon system such as the standard (51 calibre-length) 105mm gun.

The most widespread objection to this is, surprisingly, based neither on loss of flexibility nor on putting the section at undue risk by mounting them in a 'tank', but – despite a doubling in the number of kinetic energy guns – on the loss of the cannon and high-angle types of firepower. I therefore later came up with the infantry fighting vehicle outlined above, mounting a cannon and a low-pressure 76mm (as on Scorpion) capable of both low and high-angle fire, as well as a machine gun. This vehicle would have a 'command and support' variant and be grouped with a fixed gun tank destroyer (mounting a 72 calibre-length 105mm or the German 120mm smooth-bore) and a 'fire support tank' mounting externally a standard 105mm (or again the 120mm). Then of course there would be an air defence vehicle and minor variants. With the major weapon platforms and the in-house infantry's vehicle in the same family, the logistic and training arguments go the way of the rest.

One can in fact design a 'composite armoured regiment' based on this family at a strength about that of a standard infantry battalion at war establishment. This unit, in which I at least would see the composite squadron as the key tactical group, has both tactical balance in the accepted sense and a preponderance of 'tank' guns. Thanks to the saving in 'back teeth' manpower resulting from integration, the regiment has roughly the tactical worth of a conventional regiment/battalion group. I have written elsewhere about how a balanced close-combat force of composite regiments and standard or 'light' (*cf. Jäger*) battalions might fit rather neatly into the British regimental structure.

However, the final assault on the current mechanized infantry concept is a horse of quite another colour. When one examines the all-singing, all-dancing, air-

(Above) The American XM-723 IFV; this was the prototype for the later Infantry and Cavalry Fighting Vehicles

(Below) The American M2 Bradley Infantry Fighting Vehicle, armed with a 25 mm Hughes Chain gun automatic cannon

mechanized response to the predicted threat, one is struck by two related drawbacks. One is that the cost of such a force in money and high-grade manpower is intolerable to all countries except superpowers desirous of going onto the strategic offensive. The other is that, to be sure of containing the predicted threat within the confines of, say, the European theatre, the defender needs to be so strong that militarily he should not be on the defensive at all.

One wonders whether a much cheaper and more effective defence could not be provided by substantial forces of infantry on their feet, conducting a quasi-guerrilla campaign of tank-hunting, ambushes and other forms of harassment, backed up by the ability to mass fire intensively, rapidly and over long ranges by PGMs and rotary and fixed-wing support. Mao Tse Tung, Ho Chi Minh and Che Guevara – or if you prefer it Cuba, Vietnam, Afghanistan, Nicaragua and El Salvador – have many lessons to teach. But a policy of this kind requires a whole-hearted renunciation of the offensive use of organized ground forces in furtherance of one's own political aims – a change of heart which Britain, France and Germany still have to make.

100 Years Ago

Ian V. Hogg

≠ 4059 Carriage, Garrison, wrought-iron, sliding, smooth-bore, B.L., 32-pr, 42 cwt (Mark I)
Platform, wrought-iron, traversing, smooth-bore, B.L., 32-pr, 42 cwt (Mark I)
Approved 31 May 1881.

≠ 4066 Ordnance, cast-iron, smooth-bore, B.L., interrupted screw, 32-pr, 42-cwt (Mark I)
Approved 17 June 1882.

≠ 4070 Shot, smooth-bore, B.L. Gun, Case, 32-pr (Mark I).
Contains 80 8-oz sand shot and 80 mixed metal balls 16 per lb, the interstices being filled with clay and sand.
Approved 25 June 1881.

The above paragraphs from the *List of Changes in War Material and of Patterns of Military Stores* for 1882 should convince anyone who is in doubt that the

The 16 in rifled muzzle-loading gun on its proof mounting at Woolwich Arsenal butts

breech-loading smoothbore is not something recently invented by Soviet tank designers. On the other hand, perhaps it is worth some explanation, since the approval of a smoothbore just at the time that rifled breech-loaders were about to sweep the board appears to be the usual dead hand of the Ordnance Board stultifying progress. Far from it; in this case it was a perfectly logical and practical solution to a specialist problem.

The problem was the close-in defence of the many forts which were distributed around the British Isles and the Empire. These had been built in the previous 20 years, generally to the 'modern polygonal' plan, a five- or six-sided figure with 'caponiers' at the angles. These were masonry buildings which extended from the wall of the fort into the surrounding ditch; they were pierced along both sides with loopholes and were to be manned by riflemen who could then direct their fire along the ditch and the foot of the walls to deter any assaulting party.

Some time in 1879 it was decided that musketry alone was not sufficient to stop a determined assault, and that

(Below) Crown Hill Fort, Plymouth; a caponier covering the ditch. The two lower apertures were for 32-pounder guns, the upper slots for musketry

(Bottom) Fort Brockhurst, Portsmouth; the interior of a caponier showing the firing port for the 32-pounder gun and, above, firing slots for musketry. The musketry gallery has been removed

(Right) The 6 inch gun as it stood in coast defences around the Empire in 1900

something more drastic was needed. The contemporary muzzle-loaders, the only guns small enough to go into the caponiers, were too slow to be re-loaded, and so the breech-loading 32pr gun was invented. This was the existing 32pr muzzle-loader of great antiquity, converted to an interrupted thread breech with steel cup obturation. It was issued with the case shot described above, and caponiers in forts had special gun-ports cut through their masonry to allow the new gun a suitable field of fire.

They remained in service, without ever being put to warlike use, until December 1920 when they were 'to be reported for disposal, except at out-stations where they may be in use as time, signal or alarm guns, in which case they will be retained until replaced.'

4064 Ordnance, B.L., 6-inch, 80 cwt (80-pr).
Drawings of the above-mentioned gun, with its sights and fittings, have been sealed to govern a special supply of a certain number of guns for naval service . . . which is of the design and manufacture of Sir W.G. Armstrong & Company.
Approved 25 Feb 1882

4079 Ordnance wrought-iron, rifled M.L., 16-inch, 80 tons (Mark I)
Drawings sealed to govern manufacture.
Approved 23 March 1882.

Devil's Gap Battery, Gibraltar, with one of the few 6 inch guns which remain in place, deactivated, as a tourist attraction

Two notable guns made their appearance in 1882; the first of these was the breech-loading 6-inch designed by Armstrong, the ancestor of an extremely long line of 6-inch guns which have now served the British Army and Navy for a century and some of which were widely exported to foreign navies in pre-1914 days. The other was one of the largest muzzle-loaders made and was developed in answer to an Admiralty demand in 1873 for a gun to defeat 20in (51cm) wrought iron armour at 3000ft (914m) range. They were designed as turret guns and were used on (among others) HMS *Inflexible* (who bombarded Alexandria with them) and HMS *Thunderer* (who double-shotted one and blew it to pieces). In the Land Service there were two, in the armoured turret at the end of the Admiralty Pier at Dover, and these are still in position today.

Present-day ordnance engineers will be interested to know that the cost of the 16-inch gun in 1882 was £10 084, and the cost of a single round of ammunition was £26 12s 0d.

≠ 4147 Heliographs, 5-inch
Service pattern now settled.
Approved 11 Sept 1882.

Signalling was attracting a good deal of attention in the early 1880s, particularly in India where distances were long and the use of semaphore or morse flags involved innumerable relay stations. Sunlight, however, was freely available and the heliograph was invented – but by whom is uncertain. The working principle of the heliograph was that of a mirror capable of being tilted by a key. A secondary mirror collected the sun's rays and focussed them on to the movable mirror, which was aligned on the distant point.

Operating the key caused the main mirror to flash the reflected sunlight, so allowing morse code messages to be sent. It had great range; distances of up to 70 miles (113km) have been recorded. It also had the virtue of being impossible to jam and of being reasonably discreet since anyone more than a few yards away from the sight line would not see the flashes. But when the sun went in, silence descended.

≠ 4085. Pot, India-rubber, chamber.
A pattern of this article has been sealed to govern supplies for the use of lunatics, and to replace the present gutta-percha pots (≠2531) which will at once be exchanged. The new pattern is made of vulcanised india-rubber, and has been introduced, on the recommendation of the Commissioners of Lunacy, in consequence of its being softer, and therefore safer, as the previous pattern became so hard as to render it a possibly dangerous weapon of offence.
Approved 10 May 1882.

This has to be the finest paragraph ever published in 'List of Changes'. One is inclined to think that if a man was not a lunatic when he received a rubber chamber pot, he certainly would be after trying to use it.

The Current State of the NATO Alliance

Nicholas Stethem

A commonplace sight in German towns and villages, NATO training exercises

In June 1982, Canada's Prime Minister Pierre Trudeau, honorary president of the first NATO heads of government meeting since 1978, attacked the alliance for its lack of common strategy in dealing with East-West problems, and added insult to injury by denouncing the communique issued by the assembled leaders as 'cooked', a document full of cliches and 'weasel words'. This apparent peevishness on the part of of a politician who has never before this shown any particular affection for NATO besides, it would appear that all is not well in the western alliance. To judge by the events of 1982, the most curious thing about the

North Atlantic Treaty Organization is not that it is in a state of crisis, but, at the advanced age of thirty-three years, that it is still in any state at all.

It is impossible to imagine Chairman Leonid Brezhnev and his cohorts involved in the sort of furious public debate over everything from defence spending to nuclear policy which has characterized his opposition over the past few years. Although distinctly lacking in virtue, if only because of its tendency to sort out internal disagreements by invading its own members, the Warsaw Pact Organization which groups the Soviet Union, Bulgaria, Czechoslovakia, East Germany, Hungary, Poland and Romania in a 'Treaty of Friendship, Mutual Assistance and Cooperation', possesses one great advantage: absolute unity. In terms of everything from grand strategy to the details of military procurement the WPO has acted as a bloc since it was formed in 1955, a single unit responding to the aims both political and military of its dominant power, the Soviet Union. What disagreements there may be remain behind closed doors, and such events as the departure of Albania in 1968 or occasional expressions of independence of defence policy on the part of Romania fail to dent the monolithic image recently reinforced by events in Poland.

Compared with such an adversary, NATO sometimes seems to barely merit being described as an alliance. Open the morning paper on any given day and the odds are that at least one headline will announce that the west is once again divided over nuclear weapons, or Poland, Afghanistan, Soviet advances in the Third World, East-West trade, the Soviet gas supplies for Western Europe, or whatever the issue of the day might be. Such a vision of NATO bickering in the long shadow of an implacably united Soviet bloc has inspired a growth industry in the west which revolves around the production of learned articles and academic conferences which attempt either to redesign the western alliance or create a brilliant new policy with which all can agree. But just how these observers expect a naturally rumbustious collection of democracies to unite behind a single set of strategies, no matter how elegant, is unclear.

When the leaders of NATO's member states, or their ministers, meet, they bring with them to the table sixteen different sets of political priorities shaped by a multitude of forces within the societies they represent. Each voice in the debate over any NATO policy carries

different undertones of history, geography, ideology, economics, foreign policy, social theory, and, not infrequently, of the struggle for political survival on the part of the speaker. And as if that were not enough, the speakers and the governments which they represent change with annoying regularity, swinging between left and right, and between greater and lesser degrees of competence. The discussion of complex issues in such a forum would seem to lead just about anywhere except a monolithic unity to match that of the Warsaw Pact.

Unfortunately, NATO's most pressing current problem is in part a natural result of this process. It is in danger of losing an increasing amount of public support to those groups who are crying out for what appear to be simple and straightforward answers to the often contradictory questions posed by the foreign and defence policies of their respective governments. At the extremes of the political spectrum there is a powerful

A Canadian machine-gun team, laden down with the tools of their trade, pictured while taking part in the NATO exercise Fallex 81

NATO must be prepared to fight in a wide range of conditions and climates from the Aegean to the Arctic Circle. Here Canadian infantrymen man a defensive position during winter warfare exercises in Norway.

desire to simplify, once and for all, the complex and changing balances of international relationships as they have developed over several decades: on the left, for example, there is the demand for a world made simpler through nuclear disarmament and the apparently reasonable ideals of the peace movement; on the right there is a matching call for a resolution of the contradictions in the simplicity of hard and fast policies based on absolute principles and overwhelming strength.

The complex arguments which lead to such NATO decisions as the deployment of intermediate range cruise missiles or the increasing of conventional force strength at great economic cost do not stand up well in the public forum against the simplicities of the peace marchers – why deploy new nuclear weapons when we are trying to reach disarmament agreements, and why spend millions on a new fighter aircraft when that money could feed starving children? Strategic arguments do not fare well against the spectre of starving children or, particularly in Europe which is seen as the place it will happen, visions of Armageddon. At the same time, the intricacies of pulling together the policies of sixteen states with different economic interests, varying philosophies of government, and in different geographic positions relative to the threat – the view of the Soviet threat is naturally different from Bonn than it is from Washington – are beyond the patience of the right, particularly in the United States.

Such arguments are not new. The disarmament movement is older than NATO itself, and the ban the bomb movement was strong in the 1950's; the simplicities of the right are equally long in the tooth, having reached absurdist heights with the idea of bombing the Russians back into the stone age not long after the alliance was formed. What is new is the development of a broader popular base for more moderate versions of these positions. General dissatisfaction with the performance of western governments in the economic and social as well as foreign and defence fields has helped to create a coalition of popular dissent, linking opponents of nuclear power, advocates of liberal social reform, the ecological movement, old guard left wing movements and others with the various and often diverse groups opposing nuclear weapons, defence spending, membership in NATO and so forth. On the right, a similar impatience with the failures of past liberal social and economic policies in virtually all areas gives a larger constituency to those more extreme critics who wish to tip the military balance firmly in favour of

NATO, without regard for the niceties of alliance politics. Thus, through the interrelationship of issues at both extremes, the western alliance is faced with the growth of politically significant minorities in its member countries which want to change its basic nature and which have no patience with either complex strategic argument or the delicate balances through which NATO manages to minimize disagreement.

Therefore, when Chancellor Helmut Schmidt sits down to discuss an issue like theatre nuclear weapons with President Ronald Reagan, he must consider not only the official policy which he and his cabinet have devised but also the dissent against that policy represented by the peace movement in West Germany which can be in turn, a powerful influence on the left wing of his own political base, the Social Democratic Party. In turn, President Reagan's position must take into account the demands of the extreme right wing of his own Republican Party that he act decisively, without compromise, to rebuild a position of strength and American supremacy, and, if necessary in the face of allied objections, that he act unilaterally. Although this is an oversimplification, such pressures resulting from the politically significant shift to the extremes are felt by all western leaders in varying degrees.

These pressures are increased as a result of another major problem, the growing complexity of the global strategic issues facing the western alliance. The number of sovereign states in the world has tripled since NATO was conceived.

Since the late 1960s, the Soviet Union has developed the ability to extend its power on a truly global scale. Economic power, too, has begun to shift, giving the western states an even greater interest in the fates of such areas as the Persian Gulf, groupings such as the Association of South East Asian Nations, resource-rich

Iroquois class destroyers, a fleet replenishment tanker and Sea King helicopters pictured during exercises in the Caribbean, away from traditional NATO operational areas

regions like Southern Africa, and of course, the industrial giant, Japan, which is now justly, if somewhat inaccurately, included in the grouping we call 'the West'. The balance of power between east and west has become more than a matter of the nuclear balance or of relative Warsaw Pact and NATO strengths in some possible future conflict – the fate of a country as remote from the Central Front as Afghanistan is now of vital concern.

This leads to another set of potential disagreements between the Allies. Differences in trade patterns, historic spheres of influence, political philosophy and so forth lead quickly to differences in the perception of developments outside the immediate NATO area. Any attempt to generate 'a western response' to a particular problem must overcome differences in national priorities, sometimes radical differences in diplomatic style and rhetoric, and the tendency on the part of some political leaders to use the world stage for the benefit of the home audience, stepping out of the hard tangle of domestic problems to shine as the great statesman, mediator, or strategist. Even when ends are agreed upon, the means may differ – Camp David versus the Venice Declaration as routes to peace in the Middle East, for example – and when means are agreed, efforts in support of them may diverge and conflict as in the case of sanctions against the Soviet Union over Afghanistan.

And finally, even when there is agreement and the allies forge ahead more or less together, the politicians must return home and sell the western position to the voting public which, if it is aware of the country or the crisis under discussion at all, is probably having difficulty sorting 'the good guys from the bad guys' – Marxist rhetoric may pour forth from the leaders of countries with absolutely no sympathy for the Soviet Union, while revolutionaries espousing the highest democratic ideals move firmly into the Soviet camp, and governments espousing the western cause indulge in forms of repression reminiscent of Stalinism at its worst. In the confusion the voices of the growing minorities at the extremes, with their apparently simple answers, grow louder.

Ideally, the task of national leaders in handling the twin problems of complexity and the political demand for simplicity would be made easier if western heads of government were seen to agree in forums like NATO. Alliance disagreements simply add another layer of confusion to the national debate. Unfortunately, disagreements in one form or another have been a fact of alliance life since 1949.

The alliance's overwhelming strength and apparent unity during the first dozen years of its life resulted more from the accidents of history than from its intrinsic qualities and collective wisdom. Flattened by the Second World War, and well behind in the development of nuclear weapons and delivery systems, the Soviet Union did not develop a *real* challenge to overwhelming American power until well after the Cuban crisis and yet, with its takeover of Eastern Europe, with the fall of nationalist China and conflicts in Greece, Korea and Southeast Asia, the emerging Soviet bloc provided a fresh and visible impetus to western unity.

Western Europe, dependent upon American strength, aid and goodwill during its own rebuilding process tended to accept American political dominance

Canadian F-5Bs taking the role of aggressors during Exercise Maple Flag air combat training at Nellis AFB, spring 1982. These exercises gave unrivalled training experience in air to air fighting for NATO pilots

within the alliance, but then as now the further an issue was removed from the single point of common agreement – that a Soviet threat to the alliance partners exists, and that it demands a collective defence – the greater the potential for disagreement. Current disagreements over the right approach to strategic problems outside the NATO area, such as the Middle East, or, closer to home, the exact response to the acknowledged Soviet threat can be matched against the bitter divisions of the Suez Crisis and the determination of France to develop a policy and a nuclear force independent of that of the United States, leading to an eventual withdrawal from NATO's military structure. European ambivalence over American strategies in the Third World can be seen as an ironic reversal of American ambivalence towards the postwar European empires, while, on a much more mundane and technical level, the standardization of military equipment which one might expect to exist in any sensible alliance remains the problem now that it was then.

The apparent disarray which currently marks both NATO and the western alliance in general would seem, therefore, to be less a function of the fact that differences exist over specific issues, than the fact that the west's historic ability to find compromise in, or at least to work around, disagreement appears to have faltered. The increased splintering of support for national foreign and defence policies resulting both

from the movement to political extremes and the increasing complexity of the international situation have made the design of any multilateral hybrid of national policies infinitely more difficult. At the same time, the global nature of present strategic problems, and the rapidity with which the situation can change, is placing much greater demands upon both national and multilateral policies.

This last factor has caused many observers to call for the reform of the whole western system of consultation on strategic matters either through changes in the nature of the NATO system, or through the creation of some other formal structure, similar perhaps to the annual economic summits, to generate common approaches to international political problems. These proposals might have some merit if the central question was simply a matter of creating a mechanism for planning, coordinating and expressing – as the 'voice of the west', perhaps – a united western policy. At the moment, however, it is difficult to see the western states agreeing on any changes to the consulting mechanisms, let alone agreeing to common policies once they are in place. Rather than creating unity, any formal restructuring of the multilateral system might simply institutionalize disunity, and, given the expectations that would be raised on the part of both friend and foe, could leave the west in even more apparent disarray.

The Central Front remains NATO's main concern and where the burden of defence falls heaviest. Here a Canadian APC crosses a bridge built by US Army combat engineers over the Main-Donau canal

What is needed now is some means of restoring the ability to work around conflicting national policies which does not involve tinkering with the formal alliance structure, which does not blow back into national policy debates thus further complicating the problem, and which does not raise expectations of concrete results in any quarter. The aim of the exercise would be to reduce inadvertent and unnecessary disagreement, to provide early warning of developing policies which may conflict, to exchange information about national political facts of life, both noble and ignoble, which may determine a government's course or modify its rhetoric, and finally, to give the leadership of each state more time to judge and digest mutually shifting positions within the alliance before the whole issue explodes into public debate.

In sum, the aim would be informally, quietly, and if possible, invisibly, to increase the room for manoeuvre on the part of each ally before the pressure of events forces the statement of national policy.

Regular but informal meetings of alliance foreign ministers might offer one means of achieving this aim. With a broader purview than defence ministers and more able to dodge the pressure of public attention and expectation than heads of government, the foreign ministers could get together on a regular basis to extend the process of informal consultation that already exists. Meeting with no greater purpose than simply to talk about things in general, without the usual phalanx of officials and battery of agendas, without statements or communiques, this forum might offer both the opportunity and the unaccustomed leisure to discuss the gritty political realities with which each of them must deal, and to compare notes on naturally different national perceptions of international situations. The information thus shared whould then return to national governments to be inserted into policy discussions directly at cabinet level, while, ideally, from a public point of view, absolutely nothing is seen to happen, as was expected: the ministers got together, had lunch, had dinner, played golf and went sailing; all in all, it was a boring non-event.

Ideally, such an arrangement might serve to midwife agreement within the alliance, but, given the real differences that exist between the sixteen different NATO states, and between the European and American wings of the alliance in 1982, this outcome is unlikely, at least in the short term. By meeting its more limited aims, however, it would assist national governments in handling the internal political debates and the strengthening voices at the extremes of left and right which reduce their room for manoeuvre in the international forum, and which make it increasingly difficult to maintain support for those alliance policies upon which, after the expenditure of much effort and political capital, they have already managed to agree.

There is little that the alliance can do about the increasing complexity of its international environment, and as a grouping of democracies it can never hope to achieve, short of war, the sort of unity that any sensible strategist would consider vital before even considering the policy direction that this unity should then take. But NATO, at the political level, can and must become more of an asset and less of a liability in the debate over the future of foreign and defence policy that is going on in each of its member countries – the continuing argument that is the essence of the western alliance may not be able to make life easier for national governments at the moment, but it can certainly avoid making life more difficult. Failing this, NATO may find itself, in the 1990s, of interest only to historians.